Politicized Medicine

The Foundation for Economic Education, Inc.
Irvington-on-Hudson, New York

First printing June 1993
ISBN 0-910614-87-3
Copyright © 1993 by
The Foundation for Economic Education, Inc.
Irvington-on-Hudson, NY 10533

Table of Contents

III. THE INAPTITUDES OF POLITICS

Introduction

Many opponents of nationalized medicine question its workability while surrendering the foundation upon which it would rest. They yield the very premise on which all tyranny rests: the right of some individuals to control others. They subscribe to the notion that certain services are the proper concern of government, which must control and regulate them, or even provide them for the benefit of all. While they embrace the principle of political control of some industries, and political readjustments of individual income and wealth, they find it disturbing when politics finally turns its attention to their particular profession. "But we are different," they tell us. "Medical care is too important to be subjected to bureaucratic regulation and control. Its quality will decline and its expenses will soar."

Such arguments are not persuasive once you accept government as the regulator of our economic affairs and the guarantor of economic well-being. There are differences between public education and public health. But if government is expected to provide the former because public education is said to be so beneficial for all, why should government not provide an equal, or even more beneficial, service to public health? If an army of public school teachers can render valuable services to public education, cannot an army of physicians, under similar employment conditions, render equally valuable services to public health? There are technical differences: the education of our children is imparted collectively to small groups assembled in public buildings, while medical care in most cases is provided individually in non-public buildings. A surgeon operates on patients one at a time. But such differences do not explain why government should be more concerned about education than it is about medical care.

In the United States, government pays for all or part of the medical care for some 70 million persons—veterans, Medicare and Medicaid recipients, members of the armed forces, and others. Thus, government is already providing limited nationalized medicine to vast numbers of people. If this is fair and equitable, if this is a proper function of government for 70 million people, why should it be so outrageous for 250 million Americans?

The answer is simple: one practice is as bad as the other. But the multiplication of government services to more and more people is multiplying the evil, which must prevail in the end. This is why we should regret and oppose each and every step toward a provider society, the national education system as well as a national health system, and all others.

We should deny the philosophical premise of the welfare state that education, medical care, and the like ought to be available to all as a matter of right. There is no such right in nature nor in the realm of human action. The right to services and benefits, which so many are proclaiming today, is merely the right to seize income and wealth from other individuals through the body politic. The right of one is the duty of another, the benefit of one is the loss of another. The right to services and benefits actually is the right to tax and confiscate, which not only negates someone else's rights to his own labor and freedom, but also jeopardizes peaceful and harmonious social cooperation. A society that creates such rights becomes a conflict society in which political might is the source of all rights. And the rights of some become the tyranny of others.

The physician who readily accepts the transfer system in education, transportation, communication, or urban redevelopment must find it very difficult to prove why medical care should not be redeveloped according to similar plans. The dentist who, as a student at a state college and state dental school, applauded massive redistribution through public education, cannot logically oppose more transfer through public dental care.

But who wants to be logical in such matters? The physician who clamors for a million-dollar federal grant to his community hospital may resent the half-million dollar grant to the new community center. The industrialist with a multimillion dollar federal loan may be indignant about the food stamps that enrich the idle paupers. And the Social Security beneficiary who is anxiously awaiting another raise is loudly condemning federal aid to higher education. In the end, they all may perish in the sinking ship, even the innocent passengers.

To defend individual freedom successfully we must rally to the defense of all professional and economic freedoms. To reverse the long trend toward political power and economic conflict, we must turn away from government as a convenient source of rights and benefits, and once again rely on individual effort and initiative to solve our problems. And lest we be suspect of insincerity in the defense of freedom—that we seek it whenever it presumably favors us, but prefer government regulation and control whenever they promise benefits to us—we must be uncompromisingly consistent. In particular, we must show the way by shunning and relinquishing all rights and privileges that favor our own profession. The college professor must reject the Federal research grant offered to him, and the physician the Federal subsidy to the community hospital.

Some government favors were granted in the distant past, which are now taken to be unquestioned prerogatives of the profession. Old license and accreditation procedures force the student of law to attend a school accredited by the American Bar Association, and then seek admission to a state bar after passing a mandatory state examination. The procedure anchored in state legislation shelters the attorneys in each state from competition not only by unlicensed practitioners but also by other attorneys properly licensed in other states. Of course, the legislation was passed in order to safeguard and improve the quality of legal services to the citizenry. But unfortunately it also greatly reduces the number of attorneys available in each state, necessitates more labor reaching across state lines, and otherwise raises the costs of legal services and the incomes of the properly trained and licensed attorneys at law. While we need not question the motivation of the quality legislation, its effects cast doubt on the stated objectives of bar associations and their recommendations for further legislation toward professional improvements.

To question the state license procedures for schools, members, and their places of work is like questioning the very existence of the profession. But where government is the acknowledged author of license and livelihood, it can also author a national health system.

—HANS F. SENNHOLZ

I. THE RIGHT TO COMMAND

The Economics of Medical Care

by George Yossif, M.D.

In voluntary markets, private medicine included, the key knowledge necessary for trade is conveyed by freely fluctuating prices. The price system conveys knowledge of the personal and subjective utilities of the actors, that is, of the supply and demand of various commodities and services, which cannot be compared otherwise. Demand for ordinary medical care in voluntary markets is highly elastic and medical care by physicians is largely optional, except for some categories of life-threatening conditions, few in number and low in incidence, sometimes known as "catastrophic illness." As history shows, medical care in essentially voluntary markets tends to be accessible and affordable. Sustained price inflation in medical care is always a result of direct or indirect political intervention. The lately much-touted competition between providers is not the genuine competitive bidding for the satisfaction of the actual consumer of care, the patient, as a free market would have it. On the contrary, this politically created competition will further enhance and centralize the bureaucratic controls on medical care, thus compounding, instead of reducing, the inflationary effects of the multiple and pervasive political interventions already in operation.

The Voluntary Market

This pattern of trade refers to the exchanges that take place between consenting parties, free from coercion, whence the more familiar term of *free trade*. Mutual advantage for the trading parties follows necessarily, since neither would consent to the exchange if some form of gain were not expected. For free trade to exist, the obvious preliminary condition is that the participants in the exchange be the legitimate owners of the goods and services exchanged, since only the owners can legitimately dispose of property. This is why regulation of trade by

George Yossif, M.D., Ph.D., is in the practice of psychiatry. This essay appeared in the July 1985 issue of *The Freeman*.

parties other than the owners amounts to various degrees of expropriation and involuntary servitude.

Medical care is a type of individual service consisting of skilled assistance to a person's recovery from illness. The essence of this recovery is an inherent process of self-healing which cannot be supplanted, but only *assisted* (or induced, or promoted) by human interventions. The provider of such skilled assistance is usually called a physician, and the receiver a patient. Medical care also includes some types of assistance to manage chronic conditions, some types of disease prevention, and some incidental activities (such as relief of pain). It does not include assistance to terminate life or induce disease, or the conversion of humans into industrial products and major invalids.

Medical care is far from being a high priority in voluntary markets, except on rare occasions. For the most part and in most individuals it ranks way below nourishment, sanitation, education, entertainment, and so on. Most medical treatments can be deferred for various periods of time, and spontaneous healing often takes place. Lifestyles markedly affect the susceptibility to illness and the ability to heal. Effective help in case of illness can be, and often is, provided by family and friends. One's general practitioner can provide most of the professional medical care for affordable fees, or he can refer the patient to specialists he deems competent and affordable. Further, friends, acquaintances, books, and advertisements provide a wealth of both general and specific information about diseases, emergencies, medicines, and specialists. Even tentative choices made under pressure or away from home can later be converted into preferred choices.

Let the Customer Choose

Thus, the paternalistic idea that the patient or his family cannot make a proper choice of medical care because they are too ignorant or too worried to explore the market is utterly false and has been promoted by bureaucrats and some physicians for the egregious purpose of portraying themselves as indispensable. It also follows that ordinary medical expenses are not an insurable risk. They are too optional and too affordable, while the respective illnesses are too preventable and too subjective to provide an actuarial basis. Insurance for catastrophic medical expenses would be the only viable medical insurance on the free market.

In voluntary markets, the patient's *freedom of choice* is necessarily complemented by the providers' *freedom to compete*. Thus, the patient obtains the best medical care that he is able and willing to pay for, while medical fees, as well as the medical technology prices, tend to drop overall.

Yet, lower prices are not necessarily the winners in the free market. For one thing, medical services are seldom comparable between practitioners, because of differences of training, experience, manner, skill, judgment, reliability, discretion, and the like. For another, idiosyncratic intangibles, such as a familiar waiting room and set of fellow patients, a distant office picked for its closeness to a shopping mall, an attraction for the specific psychopathology of the physician or the staff, often can and do make the patient choose the apparently more expensive alternative, which is, however, a very different product from the impersonal manipulations which bear the same name in the "Emergency Room" next door.

There is little doubt that banning competition or success in the marketplace makes for a hampered, non-free market condition. But the reverse is not true; that is, competition (especially if imposed) does not necessarily lead to a free market. Gladiators, who were slaves for the most part, used to compete fiercely for victory in combat sports. And many of us compete just as fiercely for government handouts. Neither of these types of competition has led to free markets, but the difference is, of course, in the fact that victorious gladiators were freed every now and then, while those of us who win the handouts wind up with even more government controls.

In a monetary economy, advanced specialization of labor and rapid accumulation of capital become possible if prices fluctuate freely, to reflect the otherwise immeasurable utilities of the myriad actors in the market. Contrived price stability, such as wage and price control, is the deadly enemy of the essential tool of the free market, *economic calculation*. *Capitalism* is the nickname of freedom in the marketplace, because it leads to capital formation and growth, which means less labor and more leisure, capital goods of increasingly higher order, consumer goods of increasing newness, variety, and abundance.

Capitalism is thus the market arrangement which provides for the honest channeling of the *profit motive,* the motive of acquiring better value than the value given up in exchange. While still in good health, private medicine was a superb illustration of the success of capitalism.

In medicine, even more than in any other areas of human action, any third party is profoundly unable to guess the utility of any service to the actual recipient, or the costs incurred (in terms of forgone opportunities) by those who pay the bill. The bureaucrat learns nothing from the diagnostic and procedure codes, because they cannot communicate the very thing they are supposed to: the value of the medical service rendered.

Involuntary Markets

Markets are hampered if the market actors are prevented, through the use or threat of *physical force,* from acting according to their own trade decisions, or if the information on which they have to base such decisions is deliberately scrambled, through various forms of *fraud,* by some other people who, thereby, acquire property or use of at least a part of what the first group *involuntarily* gives up. Those in the first group are the *victims* of the *invaders* from the second group. In involuntary markets many people switch back and forth between these two roles.

From the standpoint of the natural law, invasion is unjust and injustice is criminal. Either the property of the victim or its use, including the possible irreversible use, is seized by the criminal, for his own or his friends' benefit. The harmony, coherence, and efficiency of the voluntary exchange are disrupted and replaced by conflict, fragmentation, and waste.

Private criminals hamper the markets illegally. But governments can pass laws to protect themselves and their friends from criminal and civil liabilities, whenever they resort to force or fraud to interfere with the free market. As they exceed their only legitimate function, that of defending the natural rights of the individual, governments have to resort to force, fraud, and an expanding body of statutes to make such actions legal.

Socialist and communist governments expropriate their subjects outright. The more insidious *Welfare State,* a pseudo-democratic version of older forms of *paternalistic despotism,* obtains the same end result through *regulation, subsidies, inflation, and taxation.* And individual freedom is also lost in the process. All areas of economic activity are affected this way, sooner or later, but in this century *medicine* has been the archstone of the edifice of power of the Almighty State, behind curtains of iron and of deception alike.

In what follows here, only those government interventions will be examined in some detail which have more importantly contributed to the spiraling medical expenditures, while others will be mentioned only briefly.

Monopolies

Monopolies are grants of exclusive privilege to engage in certain economic activities, given to individuals or groups by the political power. This means that entry into a particular field of activity is prevented or made difficult by using force. The simplest procedure is to eliminate the violators and confiscate their property outright, but modern institutions are more refined.

In the case of *medical licensure,* there is first an ideological component, designed to deceive the public into believing that licensure is operated to protect the consumer, the patient. The second component is an exclusive, expensive, and time-consuming training, wherein painstaking efforts are made to inculcate in the trainee a sense of obedience, and even devotion, toward the "profession." The third component is the bureaucratic ritual of getting licensed, quite expensive when the tedious tests which precede it and the unnecessary repeat registrations which follow it are considered. Delicensure is used occasionally against the more bothersome political opponents in the profession, but only exceptionally against incompetent physicians. The fourth component is the actual use of force against those who practice without a license: Criminal penalties, including prison terms, are provided for the violators, but are seldom necessary, given the ideological processing of the minds—"brainwashing"—both within and without the profession. Indeed, as shown in the previous section, the free market can provide all the information the patient requires to purchase medical care, through directories, advertisements, referrals, word of mouth, and the price system.

The sole purpose of licensure is to prevent the emergence of uncontrolled competition. The privileged elite can thus charge premium fees, so-called *monopoly prices.* While these fees do not necessarily maximize the receipts of the individual physician, they do maximize the receipts of the profession as a whole over the long run, which is why price-cutting doctors are often ostracized or otherwise punished by their colleagues.

A second major impediment to a free market in medicine is the enormous edifice of *government subsidies*. The best known, though not usually thought of as a means of subsidizing the medical profession, is the National Institutes of Health. This name is brilliantly deceptive, because health is not at all what this huge bureaucracy usually produces. Its main products are a horrendously *expensive technology*—which serves the interests of the medical and political establishments—and a coherent body of *theoretical and methodological dogma*—which makes competition by rival schools of thought extremely difficult and even very unlikely. This major mechanism is closely coordinated with the system of government grants to the academic establishment represented by the faculties of "approved" medical schools, further complemented by grants to various medical care facilities (hospitals, clinics, HMOs) and to the patients themselves (through *Medicare, Medicaid, Veterans' benefits*), which create the "market" required by the expensive technology and methods of practice.

Incentives for Patients

The third major impediment to a free medical market has been the political creation of incentives for the patients to buy large amounts of medical care and for the physicians to push the expensive kind. Both of these mechanisms are brought into play through one of the most fiendish tricks yet invented by the insurance industry in collusion with the government: *employee benefits*. This, of course, is a system of harnessing the healthier employees and the employers to subsidize the not-so-healthy employees, as well as those who have a proclivity to abuse handouts of any kind, whether they are called "health care" or not. Enticed by apparent tax advantages, the employees are simply herded into huge populations of captive customers for the insurance industry. Moreover, employees are virtually never offered the option of taking cash instead of these benefits, that is, the possibility to opt out of the system and shop for sickness insurance in the open market. In a free market, lower prices, catastrophic insurance, and private charity would insure adequate access to medical care even for the improvident, although the current system of expectations and incentives might make the return to free market behavior very difficult for a while.

The mechanism by which even the least abusive patient's incentives are perverted is widely known as *"first dollar coverage"* and consists of insurance coverage for all sorts of minor expenses for even the most optional kinds of medical care, with only token amounts of deductible expenses. Thus, it is not surprising that in some metropolitan areas sex therapy with surrogates has been advertised as covered by "health insurance."

The mechanism by which the physician's incentives are perverted, again through the "health insurance" schemes, consists of the *more favorable coverage and preferential compensation of highly technical and expensive methods* of diagnosis and treatment, complementing the system of institutional grants and coupled with the virtual exclusion of the patient from the transaction through the so-called *assignment of benefits* to the physician. In the process, the insurance carrier (or some agent it hires) undertakes to establish allowable fees for standardized and codified diagnoses and procedures. This is the inception of *rationing* and of the bureaucratic *control of quality* in medical care. Naturally, detailed information about the patient, both medical and non-medical, has to be made available to the payer of benefits. The *confidentiality* of the consultation and treatment, the hallmark of Hippocratic ethic, *is thereby compromised*. Thus, private medical care has been replaced by impersonal procedures and a system of surveillance even before the government takes over nominally.

Other Ideological and Legislative Interventions

The escalating operation of the types of government intervention described has been facilitated by a plethora of other ideological and legislative interventions such as:

- promotion of the concept that "health care" is a human right;
- tax policies, mostly within the frame provided by the income tax system;
- creation and expansion of various public medical facilities;
- massive regulation of medical care, especially in institutional

settings, which, like taxation, is a form of expropriation of the private sector;

- protection of the inefficient and punishment of the success-ful enterprises through the arbitrary application of the body of vague statutes and incoherent court decisions known as the "antitrust law";
- the exemption of the "business of insurance" from the anti-trust law;
- massive inflation of the money supply, often through deficit-spending, gargantuan bond issues and loan guarantees.

This is an enormously complex system of fraud and waste, which serves various special interests by using the police powers of the government, especially its regulatory and fiscal powers. Some of the participants in the scheme use it deliberately for their predatory purposes. Others contribute to the operation without grasping its meaning, dedicating themselves to the avowed humanitarian goals. In a somewhat different context, V. I. Lenin referred to such unfortunates as "useful idiots." A third category of contributors consists of those who have some vague notion of the wrong they commit and who engage in contemptible attempts to demonstrate that it is not their fault, or that it could not be avoided, or that it is right, or that they are not actually doing what they are doing. There are many semi-literate artisans in this category, among them quite a few dedicated and competent physicians. The isolated rebel is barely worth a mention here, as he is either destroyed or converted to one of the three categories in good standing. As to the dupe, we all take turns at playing that role, full-time or part-time.

The humanitarian guise of medical care and, even more so, "health care," is an excellent opportunity for the politician to obtain votes and for the bureaucrat to increase his power by deficit spending in high gear, while bestowing favors to sundry friends along the way. The role played by Medicare and other federal medical programs in the growth of the federal budget, even though only partially known or acknowledged, is staggering. Furthermore, numerous areas of government intervention—such as occupational safety, clean air, food and drug safety—are health-related.

At Taxpayer Expense

These multiple interventions in the marketplace are ultimately supported by the taxpayers, by the people on fixed incomes and, more dangerously and increasingly so, by eroding the capital base of the economy, that is, the savings-investment portion of the national income. The economic decline is further accelerated by the commitment our government has demonstrated to various international giveaways. When hyper-stagflation eventually takes a definitive and deadly hold of the economy, the federal government will—messianically and presumably at our request, as expressed, for example, in the declaration of a *state of emergency by the President*—have to assume total control of the dwindling rubble and mandate the general and immediate pursuit of happiness . . . or else!

But individual liberty can be lost much earlier by regulations allegedly aimed at protecting people's life and health. On the one hand, the economic intricacies of medical care extend deeply into the most varied industries, with insurance and pharmaceuticals as the most obvious examples. On the other hand, once individual health becomes a matter of "public interest," nothing that could even remotely affect it could escape the jurisdiction of the sovereign. Clean air requirements and mandatory safety belts have been only timid inroads. "You ain't seen nothin' yet!" But rejoice! All requirements will most certainly have to serve the dignity of human life, as defined by the best government experts, naturally. If, say, the Department of Health and Human Services continually monitors your biological functions—quite remotely and privately, of course—you can rest assured that not only the public interest will be served, but your best interests also, even if you may happen not to grasp this fully now.

The Freaks

Since the price exacted by the interventions of the government in the market is huge, both in monetary terms and in terms of costs which include personal freedoms still very dear to many of us, it would stand to reason to ask the government to back out of our pockets, businesses, and private lives. It would if we asked. Some of our representatives and senators still respond to the opinions expressed by their constituencies, even though decreasingly so. The others can be formally ordered to obey, or they can be recalled. But instead, we continue to delude ourselves that we can pull it through by making the next guy bear the brunt of the "sacrifice," although it should be clear by now that we will all bear the burden, unless we manage to shake off the yoke of big government and our predatory habits together.

A rather strange instance of letting ourselves be mesmerized into delusional thinking is the recent fad for "competitive new forms of medical care" (such as PPO's, PPI's, HMO's, etc.). Their competitiveness consists of their ability to secure, or take advantage of, favorable legislative treatment, government grants, tax exemptions, and reserved markets—that is, *captive patient populations*—in exchange for their higher compliance with the rules of the sovereign or his surrogates, in particular with the *procedures-surveillance* approach to medical care.

These freak entities—*bureaucratic medicine cloaked in free market pretenses*—have absolutely nothing to do with voluntary markets, or with any genuine competitive bidding for better patient care. Presenting them as free market phenomena is an out-and-out fraud; or the expression of a delusion, at best. They are a death trap for physicians and patients alike; they spell death of individuality, freedom, and medical professionalism. To rejoice in joining them is like rejoicing in entering the gas chamber because they are playing your favorite tune.

The Best Things in Life Are Not Free

by John C. Sparks

The old song proclaims that the best things in life are free—and specifically extols such romantic items as the moon, the sky, and the flowers in spring.

The composer of these popular lyrics doubtless earned his fame and royalties, though his philosophical sentiments might not win the plaudits of classical economists who would point out that the best things derive their value from scarcity and are far from free.

A good house that may be free for the taking is extremely scarce—in fact, nonexistent. So are automobiles, automatic washers and dryers, stereophonic consoles, engineering services, the latest medical drugs, classical art, fur coats, and endless other items and services—all scarce at prices buyers would prefer to pay.

Much as we might wish to acquire freely these best things of life, a moment's reflection shows why that is an impossible dream. None of these items is handed to us by nature. None comes into being without considerable effort by persons combining skills, years of training, and savings to produce desirable products and services.

These products or services exist only because they can command a price, a price sufficient to encourage productivity by those who have the inclination. The fact that some persons are willing to pay for new hats causes scarce and valuable hats to materialize.

Many individuals, working separately or grouped in companies, try to attract those who would buy their scarce products and services. Some succeed. Some do not. And respect for the discriminating judgment of potential buyers does more to improve the quality and variety of goods and services "for sale" than does any other factor.

The composer quite properly listed love, happiness, and other intangible wonders among the best of things. It was doubtless intended that the individual respond with actions that would *earn* for him stir-

---

John Sparks is a past president of The Foundation for Economic Education. This article appeared in the April 1968 issue of *The Freeman*.

ring soul satisfactions without an outlay of cash. Several decades later, however, the song's promise has been stretched to cover not only the *philosophically* desirable objectives listed by the song writer, but many *economically* desirable products and services as well. Obsessed by desire to consume, prevailing political action attempts to bypass the essential thought, saving, and labor that produce "the best *economic* things."

Progress in Medicine

Successful performance of a scarce and valuable service is well illustrated in the field of medicine. A medical man of 1868, given a glimpse of the parade of medical accomplishments in the century to come, could scarcely have believed such miracles possible. The description of such medical treatments, drugs, and procedures would have been a marvel to him, not to mention their blessings upon millions and millions of people. Lifespans increased unbelievably; many common and formerly fatal diseases virtually wiped out; human lives blossoming that otherwise had no chance—miracles all!

Such outstanding service in saving lives and restoring health has brought substantial economic reward to many of these modern men of medicine. In addition to the monetary rewards, many have known the personal satisfaction of serving the unfortunate ones who lack the funds to pay the full price, or perhaps any price, for needed medical attention.

So phenomenal has been medical progress in the United States that one would hardly expect it to be the object of political attack. Yet a strange brand of collectivist "logic" proclaims the "right" to free services of all kinds, including medical care—not the volunteered services of generous physicians to those unable to pay—but the cold, impersonal, regimented service yielded by federal legislation. By what logic do Americans of any age expect to receive free medical care under a system of compulsion?

Some may question the use of the word "free" to describe Medicare benefits. Does not each earner of income pay his own way through the federal Social Security system for Medicare? Furthermore, the doctor's care portion of Medicare is voluntarily chosen and paid for by the citizens. How can these be called "free"?

The answer, of course, is that no service of value can be free. Medicare is not free. It has to be paid for one way or another—or the service will not be forthcoming. But in the Medicare idea is a substantial element of something that to many of our countrymen *appears* to be a free benefit—or a *partially* free benefit. They find it easy to assume that medical benefits are in unlimited abundance instead of scarce and costly. The service seems to be there for the taking. It is true that medical drugs, technical equipment, and skills are much more plentiful than in years past; yet they do not grow on trees. Manufacturers spend millions of dollars to conduct research and develop new medicines. But their resources are limited by the amount stockholders are willing to risk in the uncertainty of researching and developing a new product. Not everyone is willing or able to endure the long years of study, expense, and self-denial to become a doctor. Doctors, therefore, are scarce. And so are the allied services such as nursing. Private and public hospital boards constantly need to raise funds for expanded facilities and improved equipment. And the difficulty in acquiring such funds accounts for the relative scarcity of hospital services.

So what? What if those who are covered under the Medicare program believe that medical services are virtually free and available in great abundance—rather than *un*-free and relatively scarce? What difference does it make? They will receive the benefits, won't they—benefits they could not otherwise afford?

Consequences of Medicare

Medicare patients now receiving medical attention otherwise beyond their means will not easily be persuaded that Medicare is likely to downgrade the quality of medicine in this nation. Nonetheless, the advent of Medicare and its supplemental programs will tend toward that result.

The discipline of the market—that is, the exchange of values between persons willing to trade their scarce savings for scarce medical services—is lost or severely impaired. Individual decision-making will be displaced by government compulsion. Tragic results are sure to follow.

Keep in mind that the cost of Medicare was estimated on the low side by its proponents to render it more palatable to wavering legislators. Costs of government programs seldom are estimated accurately. Medicare ran two or three times over its original estimate in the first year. Marginal illnesses that previously would have gone unattended now call for the doctor's attention—and add to the cost of Medicare. Patients seek more frequent and more extended hospitalization—at added cost. Medical services and medical supplies will broaden in definition so that areas never intended to come under the program will be included—and add to the costs. Opportunists will flock into the program, in collusion with patients, with supplies and "semi-hospital" services and activities bordering on the fraudulent—all to become a part of the costs.

Another extra cost—overlooked by the proponents of Medicare—is the transformation of medical services, formerly performed free or at very low cost, into full price when eligible for government compensation. One doctor who "before Medicare" spent one day a week *gratis* with the residents of a home for the elderly now allows Medicare to pay him more than $1,000 for this day.

Beyond all this is the heavy cost of bureaucratic operation and the lost sense of frugality by all parties in the program—patients, doctors, hospitals, agents, and others. What incentive remains to keep the total cost reasonable? None whatsoever. The Social Security and other tax rates will continue to grow until they finally become unbearable to taxpaying salary and wage earners. Greater federal deficits will bring further inflation.

Those to Be Blamed

And there will be scapegoats. Doctors will find their fees first restricted, then fixed. Numbers of Medicare patients will be forcibly increased without regard for the number of non-Medicare patients the doctor may prefer to serve. And there will be a revision in policy concerning other doctors who originally refused to cooperate. They will be blamed for the shortcomings of Medicare, poor attitudes, and lack of uniform coverage—and will be forced to join the program.

Private hospitals also will be among the scapegoats when they seek equitable coverage of hospital costs not now allowable for reimbursement by the Medicare program.

The innocent bystanders will be those persons not covered by Medicare but in need of medical attention, attention they will not get because so much of the scarce professional time and effort has gone into red tape, restrictions, and unnecessary "doctoring." These "forgotten" people, the ineligible, self-reliant families, will have to pay *twice,* first for the Medicare of others, and then for the care of their own families, not to mention the disproportionate share of hospital overhead expense they will be charged. For such double outlay they will receive minimum time and attention from regimented doctors. This excluded group could hardly be blamed if it were to petition legislators to make Medicare coverage universal.

A further consequence of Medicare will be noted by all too few. The rate of medical growth and discovery of the last hundred years will not be maintained. Bureaucratically fixed fees will discourage the development of new surgical procedures and concepts. Difficult, time-consuming, risky, tiring, exploratory efforts will not be worth the candle under Medicare. What fee should a doctor charge for the first heart replacement operation? And why not stick instead to simple, less expensive tonsillectomies and appendectomies? Advancement in medical science is seriously threatened by Medicare.

Since the program is now law, why point to the descending path it will follow? Why spell out the terrible price that all Americans—the young and the elderly—will pay in terms of lower quality care, the deterioration of medical science, reduced numbers of intelligent young men entering the field of medicine and scientific medical research? What good is predicting the gloomy future of medicine in the United States? The eggs have been broken, the scrambling under way. Will such portrayals of Medicare's future return us to our senses? Will this discussion help bring economic understanding? Will anyone gain from this effort the courage to join in the struggle to restore freedom in this field of human activity so vital to man's well-being? I do not know.

The Effort to Improve

The attempt must be made, however, regardless of the heavy odds against any quick rescue of medicine from the dismal detour it has taken. Some day, the collectivist idea will recede, as honest and intelligent human actions beat it into retreat. Such gains, however, do not come from wishful thinking or from dire predictions of socialistic evil. Nor is it certain that they will come from the actual misery of the adverse results. Human nature is prone to accommodate to adversity which arrives gradually—as might be expected in medical affairs under regimentation.

Only a fresh and better understanding of the achievement possible in a free society will wean support away from Medicare. Persons who think they are being practical in support of government medicine might well be persuaded to transfer their allegiance to the institutions of freedom. The search for a magic political formula that will produce the best economic things is doomed to failure. New formulas will be offered after each failure—"one more try"—which will fail in turn, until human gullibility is exhausted. Then a renewed understanding of the blessings of freedom will return to the people of our land.

To spread the understanding of freedom is our task. There is no other antidote for the regimentation of government control and interference dedicated to accomplishing the impossible. Only then will medical services and products be recognized as the best things in life, but far from free. Only then will freedom of choice and freedom of exchange return to the field of medicine. Only then will it resume its jet-like speed toward new miracles of the future.

The best things of life are not free. But human freedom is the best means to attain the most desirable "things" of our lives.

The Medical Market Place

by A. R. Pruit, M.D.

What is the state of the market, what are the economic problems of the health industry today? Realistic appraisal of the current situation requires examination of the nature of the market prior to the onset of massive state intervention. So let us review the economic history of organized medicine in the United States. Was it an open market? If not, what kind of market, and what factors led to its development?

American medicine was until about 1850 a free-wheeling, highly competitive, free market industry. Like the ministry in some religious denominations today, anyone who "felt the call" was free to hang out a shingle and declare himself available. The only restrictions were those put upon him by the quality and availability of the competition, and by the favor of the customers who dictated his rewards. Similarly, medical schools were easy to start, easy to enter. These schools taught every conceivable approach to health from the orthodox to the mystic. Many of the schools of this time were organized as profit-making institutions. Some were owned by the faculty. Some were privately endowed. Some were hardly more than diploma mills. Their quality and the quality of their products ran the gamut of the quality spectrum from excellence to quackery.

It is easy to understand why many of the finest men in orthodox medicine, those dedicated to the development of medicine as a science, would feel totally dissatisfied with this seemingly chaotic arrangement. One can only applaud their desire to improve the overall quality of medicine for the public benefit. Their problem was one of implementation. How can this improvement be accomplished? Can the people, through education or any other means, ever have enough special information to be able to recognize and choose quality care out of this hodge-podge of misinformation and charlatanism? Or, is human gullibility so great, and human ability to choose responsibly so frail, that

---

Dr. Pruit, now retired, was a physician at the Hertzler Clinic in Halstead, Kansas. This article appeared in the February 1971 issue of *The Freeman*.

some means must be found to protect individuals from their own folly and to insure the delivery of what we know to be the highest quality care? Who is to be responsible: man or the state? That was their basic question. This troublesome but fundamental question lies at the root of every sociopolitical problem which faces us today. The men in medicine did not believe that man could be responsible. Their answer: the state. They believed that orthodox medicine should seek the sanction and protection of the state to help shield the people from their inability to choose responsibly.

Origin of the A.M.A.

The American Medical Association was organized in 1847 and committed itself to two proposition which, when fulfilled, would improve the overall quality of American medicine. But these same propositions led to sharp restriction of the medical market place. From a free market, it quickly changed to what many economists call a discriminatory monopoly, which simply means a market place which favors, invariably through legislative fiat, one competing group over all others. How did this come about?

The two propositions were (1) that medical students should have acquired by the time they were ready to practice a "suitable education"; and (2) that a "uniform elevated standard of requirements for the degree of M.D. should be adopted by all medical schools in the U.S." What would be "suitable" and "elevated" was to be determined by a consensus of the best minds within the organization.

Certainly, these laudable goals of themselves could have no possible bearing on medical economics. What did bear on the medical market place, however, was the method of implementing those propositions. The method was to exclude, by state intervention, all undesirable or unqualified competition: first, by licensure of only qualified M.D.'s, and second, by control, through the state mechanism, of medical school standards.

These objectives were achieved in two stages. It took the A.M.A. fifty years to convince all state legislatures that licensure was necessary, but by 1900 this goal was accomplished. The states in turn delegated the power of licensure to organized medicine through the State Boards of Medical Examiners, all of whom were practitioners of orthodox medicine. Subsequently, control of standards of medical schools was accomplished comparatively quickly following the now famous Flexner Report in 1910. With licensure already in effect, it was a simple matter to change the rules of the State Examining Boards to consider only graduates of medical schools which were approved by the A.M.A. and/or the Association of American Colleges, whose lists were identical. A short time later, these controls were extended to many of the hospitals of the country by defining standards for hospitals eligible for internship and residency programs. Today, through the efforts of the Joint Accreditation Commission, these controls have been extended to all the hospitals in the country. The delegation of these powers by the state, making A.M.A. a quasi-state agency, gave it complete control over entry into the practice of medicine as well as control over access to the nation's hospitals. It is this control over entry and access that prompts Professor Milton Friedman of the University of Chicago to call the A.M.A. the most powerful trade union in the world. Control over entry and access is also the reason other economists call the health industry a discriminatory monopoly.

Monopoly Practices

Viewed in the light of the current acute shortage of physicians, the successful argument deriving from the Flexner Report is ironical. In brief, the argument held that America was suffering from an over-production of doctors and that it was in the public interest to have fewer doctors who were better trained. It was recommended, therefore, that a substantial fraction of the medical schools be closed; that standards be raised in the remainder and admissions be sharply curtailed. This is to say, in effect, that the public should be protected against the consequences of buying medical services from inadequately trained doctors by legislating poor medical schools out of business—as if all could have Cadillacs if Fords were outlawed.

Whatever names one may apply to the industry or to the A.M.A., it is a fact that the number of doctors produced by the medical schools has remained relatively static for many years despite a rapidly increasing population. In 1910 when the Flexner Report was published there were 23,300 medical students in the United States and the total population was roughly 100,000,000. Today, there are 35,883 medical students, to serve a population of approximately 200,000,000 [1971]. The effort to upgrade the quality of medicine by controlling the standards required of medical schools has resulted in a sharp decrease in the number of medical schools available to the students. In 1910 there were 162 medical schools in the United States. By 1920 this number had been reduced to 85; by 1930 to 76; and by 1944 it reached a low of 69. It seems clear, then, that control over entry has resulted in a restricted and controlled medical market with the number of physicians, as well as the medical schools, in chronically short supply.

When Demand Exceeds Supply, Prices Tend to Rise

It is axiomatic that when demand exceeds supply, other factors being equal, the price of the good or service in demand also increases. It is also true that when standards of quality are elevated, the price of the better quality product is also elevated. A Cadillac necessarily costs more than a Ford. To know that these laws have held true in medical economics, we only need remember that the medical profession has become one of the highest paid of all the professions—thus reflecting the relatively higher costs of medical care to the general public. Ordinarily, however, one would expect, in a market where supply is so severely restricted, a much greater cost differential than there has been. The medical profession has been able to deliver quality medical care to the general public, rich and poor, at prices within the reach of any who needed care.

There were many mitigating factors which made this possible. Once the barriers to entry into the profession were overcome, the individual physician was free to practice when, where, and how he pleased. There was no Board of Directors making decisions for everyone. Competition with his fellow physicians helped to keep his prices down and the quality of his care high. Contract with each patient through "fee for service" demanded his personal involvement with the singular problems of the individual, the essential ingredient in quality medical care. The ancient Hippocratic tradition that care would be provided regardless of ability to pay was an extremely important factor. Freedom of choice by the physician and by the patient, community respect and its derivative, the sense of responsibility to the community, played important roles. The success of the system depended precisely upon the fact that it was *not* an organized business entity. There were no police committees like peer review, or utilization review. Competition, contract, and freedom of choice provided all the restraints that were necessary.

This, then, is an economic overview of the American medical system prior to the advent of government inflation of the nation's supply of money. It was not a perfect system. There are no perfect systems this side of heaven, in spite of the contrary declaration of the planners of the American utopia. But that system functioned brilliantly enough to bring American medicine into worldwide esteem. It is the very nature of this high quality but severely restricted and inelastic supply market and of the control mechanisms which sustain it, as outlined here, which make the system so vulnerable to massive intervention. At the same time, the system raises almost insurmountable obstacles in the way of those who are totally opposed to this intervention and to the philosophy which prompts it. Whoever controls entry and access has the power to control the economic destiny of every physician in the industry if he chooses to use that power.

The Impact of Inflation

Inflation is one of the most devastating, destructive, and demoralizing forces which can be imposed on a civilized society. The distortions and dislocations which it produces are so numerous and occur in such rapid succession that the adjustments and rearrangements which society would achieve under normal growth conditions now become impossible of achievement, thus creating permanent dislocations and maladjustments with social disintegration the ultimate result.

Most of the dislocations and maladjustments which are chronic problems in the health industry today are directly or indirectly an aftermath of inflation. The increase of doctors in the cities and their decline in small towns, the growth of specialists and the decline of generalists, the increase in emotional and social problems and the decline and distortion of social values and standards are but a few of the multitude of distortions and dislocations which are aggravated by, or caused by, a continuing general inflation. I mention here these effects of general inflation because of their bearing on problems to be discussed later.

For discussion purposes, the health industry can be considered as an isolated economic unit which functions within itself in exactly the same way that the national economy does. As such a unit, it is subject to the same laws of the market place. Such an economy tends toward a state of equilibrium between supply and demand, and the prices of goods and services to the consumer are reflected in this equilibrium by remaining fairly stable.

If, in this state of relative equilibrium, there is an intrusion of hitherto unavailable money, there occurs an immediate disequilibrium. In the general economy the increased demand caused by the influx of new money is met (at least for awhile) by an increase in productivity and a rise in prices, which tends to return the market toward a state of equilibrium again.

As long as the producers can profitably increase their productivity by raising their prices, then supply and demand will continue to tend toward equilibrium.

This holds true for the general economy and it holds true for the health industry as long as the inflation is general. But when a massive increase in the supply of money is suddenly injected into the isolated economy of the health industry, there is an entirely different situation. The health industry can cope with general inflation because its internal equilibrium is not greatly disturbed. However, when a secondary inflation is imposed on the industry by a sudden vast increase in the supply of money within its isolated economy, the disequilibrium which occurs between supply and demand has immediate and serious consequences throughout the industry. The medical market cannot react as the general market reacted for the obvious reason that in the general economy, supply has been relatively flexible and could adequately respond to demand; but in the medical economy, supply, particularly in the vital area of physician's services, is relatively inflexible and cannot respond adequately to great increases in demand.

Subsidies to Medical Schools

The first major intrusion of government into the health industry began with World War II and the subsidization of medical schools. This intrusion did not cause an immediate disequilibrium in the medical market. It was concentrated in the area of what may be termed a producer's market and had no appreciable direct effect on consumer demand. However, when coupled with some of the consequences of general inflation, it did cause major changes in the distribution of physicians, thus affecting their supply in the vital area of service to the consumer.

The initial effect of the use of fiat money to subsidize medical schools was to cause an inflation of research activity. While this increased activity did serve to increase (inflate) our knowledge and technical ability in many areas, it had other far-reaching and less salutary effects. There was, first of all, a great increase in the size of the faculty of medical schools. With continued subsidization, and through the device of tenure, the number of teachers and research fellows tended not only to grow but to become permanent, thus greatly increasing the costs. Since the chief source of funds from the government was earmarked for research purposes, the schools tended to be diverted from their main purpose—to teach students—and to become more and more preoccupied with research. As the research programs grew, more and more physicians were diverted into research, thus adversely affecting the supply available for private practice.

The availability of fiat money in this area, along with the rapid growth of population and the increasing demand for medical services, did increase, very slowly, the number of medical schools and the total number of medical students. In 1944 there were 69 medical schools. By 1969, their number had climbed to 99. Interestingly enough, though hardly surprising, every medical school in America is now dependent upon the federal government for more than 50 percent of its income. Some, I am told, receive as much as 85 percent. The medical schools of America can no longer survive without continued government support. The total number of medical students attending the various medical schools by 1969 had risen to 35,883, an increase of about one-third over 1950. I have been unable to obtain any exact figures on the number of these graduates who enter private practice. However, John Gardner, former Secretary of Health, Education and Welfare, in his 1967 Report to the President on medical costs made this statement: "It is estimated that in the period 1950–1965 the demand for physician services increased by at least 41 percent, probably considerably more. Meanwhile, the total supply of active physicians increased by only about 31 percent, *while the supply of physicians in private practice increased considerably less*" (emphasis added).

Walter McNerney, writing recently on medical costs, calculated that: "If we double the output of American medical schools today and keep all other factors constant, it will be 30 years before we double the total number of physicians in the country."

Supply in the medical market place is, indeed, inelastic.

Thirty years of war and the continuous mobilization of huge numbers of men in the armed forces; the tremendous growth of bureaucratic health agencies, state and federal; the mushrooming of research programs in the medical schools and in the so-called "think tanks"—all of these, made economically possible only because of fiat inflation of the money supply, have increased the demand for physicians. The entry of doctors into these artificially created areas of demand has, in terms of the supply available to private practice, negated completely the increased production of physicians by the medical schools.

Controls Upset Balance Between Demand and Supply

The net result of government intervention in medical education has been (1) the federal government has gained virtual control of medical education; (2) in terms of an increasing demand for services there has been a relative decrease in the supply of physicians available to render services through entry into private practice.

The passage of the Hill-Burton Act initiated the second major intrusion by government into the medical market. The rapid increase in the number of hospitals which resulted, coupled with the growing demand for medical services generally, caused a hyper-acceleration of demand for trained auxiliary medical personnel of all kinds. Supply of personnel has not been adequate to meet the demand, and a spiral of wage increases has resulted throughout the industry. It is significant, as a reflection of this disproportionate increase in cost, that until the advent of Medicare, hospital fees were the only prices throughout the health industry which increased significantly faster than price levels in the general economy.

According to Mr. McNerney, "over 60 percent of health care costs are attributable directly to manpower." When one considers that nursing salaries have more than quadrupled in the last 25 years, that the salaries of other technicians have risen comparably, and that all wages are still rising, one can see immediately that the effect of special inflation within an industry where all technical help is in short supply is to put an exorbitant price tag on the services demanded.

With the advent of Medicaid and Medicare the already straining health market was immediately forced into a state of marked disequilibrium. In this instance, vast sums of unearned and hitherto unavailable dollars were suddenly poured into the demand side of the ledger.

The immediate effect was not just an increase in demand. There occurred a psychological hyperinflation of demand. The consumer, released from all the restraints imposed by "cost" and "afford," develops, rather quickly, a whole new spectrum of complaints which demand attention. Chronic ailments which were not disabling, with which he had lived and been productive for many years without seeking medical aid, now become more and more emergent. He begins to demand attention for increasingly trivial complaints. His calls upon the physician become more frequent and his hospital admissions more frequent. He demands more sophisticated and more luxurious services and facilities than he was willing and/or able to pay for before. The physician once had difficulty keeping him in the hospital long enough; more and more the problem now is getting him to leave. As we have already proved, with the vast and never-ending expansion of welfare programs over the past 30 years, there is no end to the growth of needs and demands when they are unrestrained.

As long as the government continues to stimulate demand, and supply remains inelastic, acute shortages will continue and wages will continue to rise. Attempts to improve efficiency further by more mechanization and increased para-medical personnel will only increase capital investment and operational costs. Physicians and hospitals, who must pay their bills or close their doors, have no choice but to increase fees and to continue increasing them with each new spiral of wage, price, and tax increases. This, in general, is the situation in the medical market today. As long as inflation continues, this will remain the situation, and no combination of managerial talent under the sun can do anything constructive about it.

Further Intervention No Cure

What happens when the medical market, as seems likely, becomes a government-controlled monopoly, administered by a politically oriented bureaucracy? It seems unlikely that the situation will improve under the least competent and least efficient form of administration which man has yet devised.

The only thing that can possibly be achieved by government intervention is a drastic reduction in the overall quality of medical care at a tremendous increase in cost to the consumer. The program will be entirely dependent on a continuation of inflation in spite of massive increases in taxation for the already overburdened taxpayer, and in spite of wage and price controls which will be applied throughout the industry. The demise of competition, the eradication of "fee for service" contract between the physician and the individual patient, the distortion of freedom of action and freedom of choice, must all have an almost lethal effect on physician motivation and incentive. The art of medicine under these circumstances must degenerate into a sterile and grossly distorted caricature. There may, for awhile, be luxury care but the element of quality will, all too often, be lacking.

Lower the Standards?

The only possible way to increase adequately the supply of physicians under the present circumstances is to lower the standards of qualification. Just as the Registered Nurse shortage of the 1950s caused the development of Licensed Practical Nurse programs, so will the planners try to meet the physician shortage by the development of what should be, but will not be, called Licensed Practical Physician programs. The imposition of these programs will, in effect, turn the clock back about 70 years, as far as the overall quality of medical practice is concerned. In the pre-Flexner Report era, however, the consumer had a free choice of quality. In our time the poor quality care will be imposed by the state. The vast majority of Americans will have to accept it. There will be no choice in the matter.

This is not a pleasant report. It is, I believe, an honest one. I cannot here attempt evaluation in depth of the many maladjustment which have accrued, not only from external influence and interference, but also from our own past errors both of omission and commission in the management of our affairs. Further study and evaluation of these fundamental problems are, in my opinion, imperative. No useful purpose can be served by minimizing a serious situation. Just how serious our situation is becomes immediately apparent when we realize that the problems of medicine are but one set of symptoms of a disease which threatens our entire social structure.

There is no easy solution. Before we can understand effects, the causes in which they are rooted must be explored and identified. Until we understand causes, we cannot hope to find effective solutions.

The situation is by no means hopeless. On the contrary, we have every reason to be hopeful. There is more awareness, more concern, more intensive study, more understanding of fundamental issues today than at any time in the past 30 years. Disillusionment with government policy, its profligate spending, its gross inefficiency, its monumental failure to improve society is growing rapidly. Inflation cannot last forever. It must end, as historically it always has, in economic and social disaster, but this will not be the end of the world. Our form of government may not survive, but we will. If we know and understand enough, we can, in our turn, and in our sphere, help recapture a heritage which we have somehow lost.

Medical Care Is Not a Right

by Charles W. Johnson, M.D.

Rights are what stouthearted men supposedly fight for. This muddled definition is probably as good as most people's understanding of this blood-soaked concept. Rights is a word which provokes emotion. Label something a right, play a martial tune, and the legions will march to your cause. If your opponents accept your sloppy definitions, victory is yours. Stouthearted men might do well to identify those rights they adore.

The concept of rights has developed over several centuries. It is a complex body of thought about the nature of man. These ideas have had consequences; they enabled man to emerge from barbarism. The concept, quite properly, has acquired an emotional value. Unfortunately, to most people, the concept is hazy, distorted by those who wish to cash in on its emotional power.

Rights, as defined by Burke and Locke, as incorporated in the Declaration of Independence, the *Federalist Papers,* and the writings of others, are the conditions necessary for man's survival according to his nature, as he was designed by God or nature. Man, in order to exist among the other flora and fauna of this planet, has certain requirements. First, he must have a drive to live and continuously act to sustain his life. By his natural design, his special means of survival are: conceptual, volitional thinking; hands designed for tools; and differentiation, enabling man to specialize his productive energy and to prosper by trading with one another, each party profiting by the exchange. The conditions such social organization requires are: the free range of each man to think, choose, and act; and to own property, to hold secure the products of his mind and hands for him to consume or save or trade. Men must, to live, assert a claim to these conditions: life, liberty, and ownership. These proper claims are rights. Actions against

Dr. Johnson practices in San Antonio, Texas. This article was reprinted by permission from the January-February 1969 issue of *G. P. Press,* published by the Texas Academy of General Practice, and appeared in the April 1969 issue of *The Freeman*.

this system, the molestation of another man's life, liberty, and property, are wrongs.

No one has a right to anything he must ask permission for or in any way take from another. In interpersonal and societal relationships there are many goods and services traded and privileges granted, but there is no "right" to take these from another. In distinguishing rights from privileges one may ask, "provided by whom?" If it is provided by God or nature or by one's own self, it is a right. If it is provided by someone else, it is a voluntary exchange, a privilege—or theft.

No one has a right to food, water, shelter, money, or love if he must obtain it at the expense of the owner. Medical care is no more a right than these.

Man rightfully obtains goods and services by producing them from nature or by voluntary exchange with others. Man may exchange goods, services, and emotional values, but he must trade to obtain them. Otherwise he is a thief acting against human existence.

Medical care is a service traded or a privilege granted—or theft.

The Right to Health

by Thomas S. Szasz, M.D.

The concept that medical treatment is a right rather than a privilege has gained increasing acceptance during the past decade.[1] Its advocates are no doubt motivated by good intentions; they wish to correct certain inequalities existent in the distribution of health services in American society.

The desire to improve the lot of less fortunate people is laudable. Indeed, I share this desire. Still, unless all inequalities are considered inequities—a view clearly incompatible with social organization and human life as we now know it—two important questions remain. First, which inequalities should be considered inequities? Second, what are the most appropriate means for minimizing or abolishing the inequalities we deem "unjust"? Appeals to good intentions are of no help in answering these questions.

There are two groups of people whose conditions with respect to medical care the advocates of a right to treatment regard as especially unfair or unjust, and whose situations they seek to ameliorate. One is the poor, who need ordinary medical care; the other group is composed of the inmates of public mental hospitals, presumably in need of psychiatric care. The propositions, however, that poor people ought to have access to more, better, or less expensive medical care than they now do and that people in public mental hospitals ought to receive better psychiatric care than they now do, pose two quite different problems. I shall, therefore, deal with each separately.

The availability of medical services for a particular person, or group of persons, in a particular society depends principally upon the

Dr. Szasz is Professor Emeritus of Psychiatry, State University of New York, Upstate Medical Center, Syracuse, N.Y. This essay, which was reprinted by permission from *The Georgetown Law Journal*, appeared in the June 1969 issue of *The Freeman*.

supply of the services desired and the prospective user's power to command these services. No government or organization—whether it be the United States government, the American Medical Association, or the Communist Party of the Soviet Union—can provide medical care, except to the degree it has the power to control the education of physicians, their right to practice medicine, and the manner in which they dispose of their time and energies. In other words, only individuals can provide medical treatment for the sick; institutions, such as the church and the state, can promote, permit, or prohibit certain therapeutic activities, but cannot by themselves provide medical services.

The Restrictive Function of the State

Social groups wielding power are notoriously prone, of course, to prohibit the free exercise of certain human skills and the availability of certain drugs and devices. For example, during the declining Middle Ages and the early Renaissance, the church repeatedly prohibited Jewish physicians from practicing medicine and non-Jewish patients from seeking the former's services. The same prohibition was imposed by the government of Nazi Germany. In the modern democracies of the free West, the state continues to exercise its prerogative to prohibit individuals from engaging in certain kinds of therapeutic activities. This restrictive function of the state with respect to medical practice has been, and continues to be especially significant in the United States.

Without delving further into the intricacies of this large and complex subject, it should suffice to note that our present system of medical training and practice is far removed from that of laissez-faire capitalism for which many, especially its opponents, mistake it. In actuality, the American Medical Association is not only an immensely powerful lobby of medical vested interests—a force that liberal social reformers generally oppose—but it is also a state-protected monopoly, in effect, a covert arm of the government—a force that the same reformers ardently support.[2] The result of this alliance between organized medicine and the American government has been the creation of a system of education and licensure with strict controls over the production and distribution of health care, which leads to an artificially created chronic shortage of medical personnel. This result has been achieved by limiting the number of students to be trained in medicine through the regulation of medical education and by limiting the number of practitioners through the regulation of medical licensure.

Supply and Demand

A basic economic concept is that when the supply of a given service is smaller than the demand for it, we have a sellers' market. This is obviously beneficial for the sellers—in this case, the medical profession. Conversely, when the supply is greater than the demand, we have a buyers' market. This is beneficial for the buyers—in this case, the potential patients. One way—and according to the supporters of a free market economy, the best way—to help buyers get more of what they want at the lowest possible price is to increase the supply of the needed product or service. This would suggest that instead of government grants for special Neighborhood Health Centers and Community Mental Health Centers, the medical needs of the less affluent members of American society could be better served simply by repealing laws governing medical licensure. As logical as this may seem, in medical and liberal circles this suggestion is regarded as harebrained, or worse.[3]

Since medical care in the United States is in short supply, its availability to the poor may be improved by redistributing the existing supply, by increasing the supply, or by both. Many individuals and groups clamoring for an improvement in our medical care system fail to scrutinize this artificially created shortage of medical personnel and to look to a free market economy for restoration of the balance between demand and supply. Instead, they seek to remedy the imbalance by redistributing the existing supply—in effect, by robbing Peter to pay Paul. This proposal is in the tradition of other modern liberal social reforms, such as the redistribution of wealth by progressive taxation and a system of compulsory social security. No doubt, a political and economic system more socialistic in character than the one we now have could promote an equalization in the quality of the health care received by rich and poor. Whether this would result in the quality of the medical care of the poor approximating that of the rich, or vice versa, would remain to be seen. Experience suggests the latter. For over a century, we have had our version of state-supported psychiatric care for all who need it: the state mental hospitals system. The results of this effort are available for all to see.

The "Right" to Psychiatric Treatment[4]

Most people in public mental hospitals do not receive what one would ordinarily consider treatment. With this as his starting point, Birnbaum has advocated "the recognition and enforcement of the legal right of a mentally ill inmate of a public mental institution to adequate medical treatment for his mental illness."[5]

Although it defined neither "mental illness" nor "adequate medical treatment," this proposal was received with enthusiasm in both legal and medical circles.[6] Why? Because it supported the myth that mental illness is a medical problem that can be solved by medical means.

The idea of a "right" to mental treatment is both naive and dangerous. It is naive because it considers the problem of the publicly hospitalized mental patient as a medical one, ignoring its educational, economic, moral, religious, and social aspects. It is dangerous because its proposed remedy creates another problem—compulsory mental treatment—for in a context of involuntary confinement the treatment, too, shall have to be compulsory.

Hailing the right to treatment as "A New Right," the editor of *The American Bar Association Journal* compared psychiatric treatment for patients in public mental hospitals with monetary compensation for the unemployed.[7] In both cases, we are told, the principle is to help "the victims of unfortunate circumstances."[8]

But things are not so simple. We know what unemployment is, but we are not so clear regarding the definition of mental illness. Moreover, a person without a job does not usually object to receiving money; and if he does, no one compels him to take it. The situation for the so-called mental patient is quite different. Usually he does not want psychiatric treatment. Yet, the more he objects to it, the more firmly society insists that he must have it.

Of course, if we *define* psychiatric treatment as "help" for the "victims of unfortunate circumstances," how can anyone object to it? But the real question is twofold: What is meant by psychiatric help and what should the helpers do if a victim refuses to be helped?

From a legal and sociologic point of view, the only way to define mental illness is to enumerate the types of behavior psychiatrists consider to be indicative of such illness. Similarly, we may define psychiatric treatment by listing the procedures which psychiatrists regard as instances of such therapy. A brief illustration should suffice.

Levine lists 40 methods of psychotherapy.[9] Among these, he includes: physical treatment, medicinal treatment, reassurance, authoritative firmness, hospitalization, ignoring of certain symptoms and attitudes, satisfaction of neurotic needs, and bibliotherapy. In addition, there are physical methods of psychiatric therapy, such as the prescription of sedatives and tranquilizers, the induction of convulsions by drugs or electricity, and brain surgery.[10] Obviously, the term "psychiatric treatment" covers everything that may be done to a person under medical auspices—and more.

In relation to psychiatric treatment, then, the most fundamental and vexing problem becomes: How can a "treatment" which is compulsory also be a right? As I have shown elsewhere,[11] the problem posed by the neglect and mistreatment of the publicly hospitalized mentally ill is not derived from any insufficiency in the treatment they receive, but rather from the basic conceptual fallacy inherent in the notion of mental illness and from the moral evil inherent in the practice of involuntary mental hospitalization. Preserving the concept of mental illness and the social practices it has justified and papering over its glaring cognitive and ethical defects by means of a superimposed "right to mental treatment" only aggravates an already tragically inhuman situation.

As my foregoing remarks indicate, I see two fundamental defects in the concept of a right to treatment. The first is scientific and medical, stemming from unclarified issues concerning what constitutes an illness or treatment and who qualifies as a patient or physician. The other is political and moral, stemming from unclarified issues concerning the differences between rights and claims.

Unclarified Issues

In the present state of medical practice and popular opinion, definitions of the terms "illness," "treatment," "physician," and "patient" are so imprecise that a concept of a right to treatment can only serve to muddy further an already very confused situation. One example will illustrate what I mean.

One can "treat," in the medical sense of this term, only a disease, or, more precisely, only a person, now called a "patient," suffering from a disease. But what is a disease? Certainly, cancer, stroke, and heart disease are. But is obesity a disease? How about smoking cigarettes? Using heroin or marijuana? Malingering to avoid the draft or collect insurance compensation? Homosexuality? Kleptomania? Grief? Each one of these conditions has been declared a disease by medical and psychiatric authorities with impeccable institutional credentials. Furthermore, innumerable other conditions, varying from bachelorhood and divorce to political and religious prejudices, have been so termed.

Similarly, what is treatment? Certainly, the surgical removal of a cancerous breast is. But is an organ transplant treatment? If it is, and if such treatment is a right, how can those charged with guaranteeing people the protection of their right to treatment discharge their duties without having access to the requisite number of transplantable organs? On a simpler level, if ordinary obesity, due to eating too much, is a disease, how can a doctor treat it when its treatment depends on the patient eating less? What does it mean, then, that a patient has a right to be treated for obesity? I have already alluded to the facility with which this kind of right becomes equated with a societal and medical obligation to deprive the patient of his freedom—to eat, to drink, to take drugs, and so forth.

Who is a patient? Is he one who has a demonstrable bodily illness or injury, such as cancer or a fracture? A person who complains of bodily symptoms, but has no demonstrable illness, like the so-called "hypochondriac"? The person who feels perfectly well but is said to be ill by others, for example, the paranoid schizophrenic? Or is he a person, such as Senator Barry Goldwater, who professes political views differing from those of the psychiatrist who brands him insane?

Finally, who is a physician? Is he a person licensed to practice medicine? One certified to have completed a specified educational curriculum? One possessing certain medical skills as demonstrated by public performance? Or one claiming to possess such skills?

It seems to me that improvement in the health care of poor people and those now said to be mentally ill depends less on declarations about their rights to treatment and more on certain reforms in the language and conduct of those professing a desire to help them. In particular, such reforms must entail refinements in the use of medical concepts, such as illness and treatment, and a recognition of the basic differences between medical intervention as a service, which the individual is free to seek or reject, and medical intervention as a method of social control, which is imposed on him by force or fraud.

"Rights" versus "Claims"

The second difficulty which the concept of a right to treatment poses is of a political and moral nature. It stems from confusing "rights" with "claims," and protection from injuries with provision for goods or services.

For a definition of right, I can do no better than to quote John Stuart Mill: "I have treated the idea of a right as *residing in the injured person and violated by the injury* . . . . When we call anything a person's right, we mean that he has a valid claim on society to protect him in the possession of it, either by force of law, or by that of education and opinion . . . . To have a right, then, is, I conceive, to have something which *society ought to defend me in the possession of.*"[12]

This helps us distinguish rights from claims. Rights, Mill says, are "possessions"; they are things people have by nature, like liberty; acquire by dint of hard work, like property; create by inventiveness, like a new machine; or inherit, like money. Characteristically, possessions are what a person *has,* and of which others, including the state, can therefore deprive him. Mill's point is the classic libertarian one: The state should protect the individual in his rights. This is what the Declaration of Independence means when it refers to the inalienable rights to life, liberty, and the pursuit of happiness. It is important to note that, in political theory, no less than in everyday practice, this requires that the state be strong and resolute enough to protect the rights of the individual from infringement by others and that it be decentralized and restrained enough, typically through federalism and a constitution, to insure that it will not itself violate the rights of its people.

In the sense specified above, then, there can be no such thing as a right to treatment. Conceiving of a person's body as his possession—like his automobile or watch (though, no doubt, more valuable)—it is just as nonsensical to speak of his right to have his body repaired as it would be to speak of his right to have his automobile or watch repaired.

It is thus evident that in its current usage and especially in the phrase "right to treatment" the term "right" actually means claim. More specifically, "right" here means the recognition of the claims of one party, considered to be *in the right,* and the repudiation of the claims of another, opposing party, considered to be *in the wrong,* the "rightful" party having allied itself with the interests of the community and having enlisted the coercive powers of the State on his behalf. Let us analyze this situation in the case of medical treatment for an ordinary bodily disease. The patient, having lost some of his health, tries to regain it by means of medical attention and drugs. The medical attention he needs is, however, the property of his physician, and the drug he needs is the property of the manufacturer who produces it. The patient's right to treatment thus conflicts with the physician's right to liberty, that is, to sell his services freely, and the pharmaceutical manufacturer's rights to his own property, that is to sell his products as he chooses. The advocates of a right to treatment for the patient are less than candid regarding their proposals for reconciling this proposed right with the right of the physician to liberty and that of the pharmaceutical manufacturer to property.[13]

Nor is it clear how the right to treatment concept can be reconciled with the traditional Western concept of the patient's right to choose his physician. If the patient has a right to choose the doctor by whom he wishes to be treated, and if he *also* has a right to treatment, then, in effect, the doctor is the patient's slave. Obviously, the patient's right to choose his physician cannot be wrenched from its context and survive; its corollary is the physician's right to accept or reject a patient, except for rare cases of emergency treatment. No one, of course, envisions the absurdity of physicians being at the personal beck and call of individual patients, becoming literally their medical slaves, as some had been in ancient Greece and Rome.

Bureaucratic Decisions and Care

The concept of a right to treatment has a different, much less absurd but far more ominous, implication. For just as the corollary of the individual's freedom to choose his physician is the physician's freedom to refuse to treat any particular patient, so the corollary of the individual's right to treatment is the denial of the physician's right to reject, as a patient, anyone officially so designated. This transformation removes, in one fell swoop, the individual's right to define himself as sick and to seek medical care as he sees fit, and the physician's right to define whom he considers sick and wishes to treat; it places these decisions instead in the hands of the state's medical bureaucracy.

As a result, bureaucratic care, as contrasted with its entrepreneurial counterpart, ceases to be a system of healing the sick and instead becomes a system of controlling the deviant. Although this outcome seems to be inevitable in the case of psychiatry (in view of the fact that ascription of the label "mental illness" so often functions as a quasi-medical rhetoric concealing social conflicts), it need not be inevitable for non-psychiatric medical services. However, in every situation where medical care is provided bureaucratically, as in Communist societies, the physician's role as agent of the sick patient is necessarily alloyed with, and often seriously compromised by, his role as agent of the state. Thus, the doctor becomes a kind of medical policeman—at times helping the individual, and at times harming him.

Returning to Mill's definition of a "right," one could say, further, that just as a man has a right to life and liberty, so, too, has he a right to health and, hence, a claim on the state to protect his health. It is important to note here that the right to health differs from the right to treatment in the same way as the right to property differs from the right to theft. Recognition of a right to health would obligate the state to prevent individuals from depriving each other of their health, just as recognition of the two other rights now prevents each individual from depriving every other individual of liberty and property. It would also obligate the state to respect the health of the individual and to deprive him of that asset only in accordance with due process of law, just as it now respects the individual's liberty and property and deprives him of them only in accordance with due process of law.

As matters now stand, the state not only fails to protect the individual's health, but actually hinders him in his efforts to safeguard his own health, as in the case of its permitting industries to befoul the waters we drink and the air we breathe. The state similarly prohibits individuals from obtaining medical care from certain officially "unqualified," experts and from buying and ingesting certain officially "dangerous" drugs. Sometimes, the state even deliberately deprives the individual of treatment under the very guise of providing treatment.

Conclusion

The state can protect and promote the interests of its sick, or potentially sick, citizens in one of two ways only: either by coercing physicians, and other medical and paramedical personnel, to serve patients—as state-owned slaves in the last analysis, or by creating economic, moral, and political circumstances favorable to a plentiful supply of competent physicians and effective drugs.

The former solution corresponds to and reflects efforts to solve human problems by recourse to the all-powerful state. The rights promised by such a state—exemplified by the right to treatment—are not opportunities for uncoerced choices by individuals, but rather are powers vested in the State for the subjection of the interests of one group to those of another.

The latter solution corresponds to and reflects efforts to solve human problems by recourse to individual initiative and voluntary association without interference by the state. The rights exacted from such a state—exemplified by the right to life, liberty, and health—are limitations on its own powers and sphere of action and provide the conditions necessary for, but of course do not insure the proper exercise of, free and responsible individual choices.

In these two solutions we recognize the fundamental polarities of the great ideological conflict of our age, perhaps of all ages and of the human condition itself; namely, individualism and capitalism on the one side, collectivism and Communism on the other.

There is no other choice.

---

1. "Concisely stated, the standard [of law as public policy] is that every individual has a right to treatment, a right to good treatment, a right to the best treatment." B. S. Brown, "Psychiatric Practice and Public Policy," *American Journal of Psychiatry*, August 1968, pp. 142–43.

2. Joseph S. Clark, Jr., then Mayor of Philadelphia, defined a "liberal" as "one who believes in utilizing the full force of government for the advancement of social, political, and economic justice at the municipal, state, national, and international levels." Clark, "Can the Liberals Rally?" *The Atlantic Monthly,* July 1953, p. 27.

3. For an excellent discussion of the deleterious effects on the public of professional licensure requirements, see Milton Friedman, *Capitalism and Freedom* (Chicago: University of Chicago Press, 1961). Friedman correctly notes that the justification for enacting special licensure provisions, especially for regulating medical practice, "is always said to be the necessity of protecting the public interest. However, the pressure on the legislature to license an occupation rarely comes from the members of the public . . . . On the contrary, the pressure invariably comes from members of the occupation itself" (p. 140).

4. This part of the article is adapted, with minor modifications and additions, from my book, *Law, Liberty and Psychiatry* (New York: Macmillan, 1963), pp. 214–16. My objections to the concept of a "right to mental treatment," formulated in 1962, seem to me as valid today as they were then.

5. M. Birnbaum, "The Right to Treatment," *American Bar Association Journal* 46:499 (1960).

6. For example, see T. Gregory, "A New Right" (Editorial), *American Bar Association Journal* 46:516 (1960); and D. Janson, "Future Doctors Chide the A.M.A., Deplore Stand That Health Care Is Not a Right," *The New York Times,* December 15, 1967, p. 21.

7. Gregory, *op. cit.,* p. 516.

8. *Ibid.*

9. M. Levine, *Psychotherapy in Medical Practice* (New York: Macmillan, 1942), pp. 17–18.

10. The following is a curious, though by no means rare, example of the kind of thing that passes nowadays for mental treatment. In Sydney, Australia, "a former tax inspector on trial for murdering his sleeping family was found not guilty on grounds of mental illness . . . . A psychiatrist told the court yesterday that Sharp, on trial for killing his wife and two children, had apparently cured his mental illness when he shot himself in the head." (*New York Herald Tribune* [Paris], July 5, 1968, p. 5.) Murder is here considered an "illness," and a brain injury a "treatment" and indeed a "cure" for it. In the Brave New World where treatment is a right, will every murderer have the right to a brain injury—if not by means of a gun, then perhaps by that of a leucotome?

11. See T. S. Szasz, *The Myth of Mental Illness* (New York: Hoeber-Harper, 1961); *Law, Liberty and Psychiatry* (New York: Macmillan, 1963); and *Psychiatric Justice* (New York: Macmillan, 1965).

12. J. S. Mill, "Utilitarianism" [1863], in M. Learner, ed., *Essential Works of John Stuart Mill* (New York: Bantam Books, 1961), p. 238.

13. The proposition that sick people have a special claim to the protection of the state—in other words, that they be allowed to use the coercive apparatus of state to expropriate the fruits of the labor of others—is a part of a much larger theme, namely, the inevitable tendency in a society for each special interest group to enlist the powers of the state on its own behalf. In this connection, R. A. Childs has recently written: "Economically, the state uses its monopoly on expropriation of wealth to create political castes, or 'classes' . . . . Thus, today, we see the state being supported by businessmen who are being benefited by defense contracts and other state patronage, tariffs, subsidies, and special tax 'loopholes' unions which are benefited by labor laws; farmers benefited by price supports; and other groups benefited by other state-granted privileges . . . . Of course, almost every group is harmed more by the benefits heaped on other groups than it is helped by its own special privileges, but since the state has gotten people to believe that the only valid approach to problems is to increase, rather than to decrease, state powers, no one mentions the possibility of benefiting each group by removing the special privileges of all other groups. Instead, each group supports the state, to benefit itself at the expense of all other groups." R. A. Childs, Jr., "Autarchy and the Statist Abyss," *Rampart Journal,* Summer 1968, pp. 4–5.

Long ago, Tocqueville had perceived this phenomenon and warned of its dangerous consequences for individual liberty. "The government having stepped into the place of Divine Providence in France it was but natural that everyone, when in difficulties, invoked its aid." Alexis de Tocqueville, *The Old Regime and the French Revolution* [1856] (Garden City, N.Y.: Doubleday-Anchor, 1955), p. 70.

Political Intervention in Medicine

by Richard E. Hunt, M.D.

In trying to define the nature of current problems in human relations it is essential first to define man's basic nature. Behavior then in keeping with this basic nature will lead to harmony and happiness in human existence, the aim of all rational, moral men.

Man is a being of volitional consciousness. He is constantly faced with the choice of thinking rationally or evading reality. Knowledge comes from his conscious perception of his environment, that is the real world in which he lives, concepts are then formed based on reality as it exists and the integration of these concepts leads to advances as yet undreamed of.

We all have only one basic right and that is the right to lead our own life and seek our own happiness. Man has sole, individual responsibility for his actions (his life) and must assume these responsibilities. We are not all equal in any ability. Each one of us is different. Each one of us has strengths and weaknesses in mind and body, and it is immoral for one to gain strength by exploiting the weakness of another; just as it is immoral for one to use his weakness as a claim on another's strength. Only through evasions, lies, and tricks is one able to avoid punishment for his errors and reward for his accomplishments. There is no status quo; there are no guarantees of success; there is no basic minimum; and by the same line of reasoning there are no limits to the productivity of men's minds under a system of free, voluntary cooperation.

Our country was founded to assure "life, liberty, and the pursuit of happiness" for all who would pursue these goals, not for any one segment of the population, not just for the politicians, not just for the white people, not just for the Negro people. We all have the right to lead our own lives. All the other things currently referred to as such

---

Dr. Hunt, an anesthesiologist in Santa Rosa, California, wrote this essay for the *AMA News,* October 28, 1968. It was reprinted with permission in the July 1969 issue of *The Freeman*.

are not rights. They are privileges. Education, automobiles, medical care, color TV, good housing, and the like are all basically produced by the conscious effort of men's minds and they must be earned by the recipients. If they are not, if they are taken by force, by legislative actions, or by lies or tricks from the people who produce them and are given to others simply because someone says he needs them, there is the immediate creation of the old slave-master relationship. In this case we have the absurd situation of the producer being the slave of the man who "needs" his product because the government has forced it to be so. The products of men's minds and labor both tangible and intangible are being taken out of the hands of the producers by political intervention in every segment of our lives.

Political intervention is responsible for the moral degradation and misery we are rushing toward. Those people in government who feel they can improve on reality, who feel they can "plan" things and do better than the law of supply and demand, are thoroughly evil and immoral because of the inevitable lowering of living standards their planning creates. It makes no difference whether they do this with conscious intent or are merely well meaning but naive. The end result is the same—misery, poverty, lack of respect for law and order, and bloodshed. I hold the politicians who advocate this intervention as well as those who would cooperate with them in the "planning," be they physicians or businessmen, personally responsible for the mess this country is in today.

Most physicians believe in free enterprise. They recognize that the affluence and high standard of living which Americans and others in the free world enjoy today is due to voluntary cooperation of thoughtful, rational men in a free market. The high standard of medical care we have today is due to the freedom under which we have practiced in the past, and most patients realize this, too. We are traders in a free market. We trade services for money which represents the productivity of our patients in their respective fields. Because our services are so important, we occupy a position of relatively greater influence in our society. We are well educated and do our best for our patients because it is in our rational self-interest and the interest of our patients to do so. We are not infallible. We are men, not gods. We make errors and we do our best to learn from them. But today the malpractice suits against doctors are attempting to penalize physicians for not being infallible! The grotesqueness of this travesty of justice staggers the imagination of any rational man.

Many people feel today that capitalism is good for the rich people, for the "Wall Street financiers," or for the privileged, and that capitalism is designed to keep the poor people in a position of subservience and poverty. Nothing could be further from the truth. This is a lie which has been furthered and nurtured *ad nauseam* by every collective political system in history both current and past. I refer now to the Nazis, all forms of Communism or socialism, and to the welfare statists and social planners in this country today.

The truth is that capitalism is the only system which has ever given every citizen a chance to improve himself and which puts a stop to coercive monopolies which tend to fix prices and wages thereby insuring that those in a lower economic position will never be able to improve their lot. Coercive monopolies, price and wage fixing, and poverty are results only of governmental interference. There is no other way it can be done except by legislation. The free market operates in exactly the opposite way and is therefore the only moral choice for rational men to make today.

With the above in mind it is with intense regret that I see the medical profession publicly demonstrate its willingness to cooperate in governmental schemes which overtly claim an interest in improving medical care. Doctors are in error who say that if the medical profession supports and collaborates with these governmental health programs, they will succeed in improving the quality of medical care. This is another way of saying that if the programs fail to live up to the great expectations of the politicians, it will be the physicians who are to blame. The programs were doomed to failure as efforts to benefit mankind, just as every other socialistic plan has caused poverty, misery, and bloodshed in the past. Only naive men would accept such blame and guilt. We as physicians in our own self-interest and that of our patients should never accept such a position whether it is placed on us by the government or by another physician. We must place the guilt where it belongs—on the men who drew up the laws and on those who support governmental interference in the practice of medicine.

Collectivism in Medicine:
An Exception or a Hook?

by Jane M. Orient, M.D.

Since the time of Bismarck, most schemes for collectivism have started with health care. Far more support can be garnered for national health insurance than for nationalizing steel factories. Many claim that medical care is not, or should not be, a kind of industry, governed by the same laws of economics as manufacturing, trade, and other service enterprises. The thought of doctors profiting from human suffering, or of a patient being turned away because of a "negative wallet biopsy," predictably arouses indignation.

Any discussion of economics in medical care is emotionally charged, because people naturally fear sickness, dependency, and death. Their fear may be exploited to cloud their powers of reasoning, making health care an excellent hook for introducing socialist ideas. Though the term "hook" (as a verb) may have entered common parlance via popular books on transactional analysis, the term (as a noun) derives from Lenin's *Thesis on Tactics*. The Communist International advises searching for and taking advantage of all sources of discontent among the masses.[1]

Is Medicine a Unique Endeavor?

Essential to the tactic of using medicine as a hook is to emphasize ways in which it appears to differ from other activities. One inherent different is asserted to be the influence of physicians on the use of services. Though physicians' fees in 1973 constituted only 19 percent of total health expenditures,[2] it is believed that "physicians are in the unique position of being able to regulate the demand for their ser-

Dr. Orient is in the private practice of medicine in Tucson, Arizona, and is the Executive Director of the Association of American Physicians and Surgeons. This article originally appeared in the June 1982 issue of *The Freeman*.

vices."[3] They order admission to the hospital, laboratory tests, drugs, and surgical procedures.

Although people can live without dishwashers and automobiles, or without hairdressers and teachers, medical care is felt to be a matter of life and death. In some cases, denying medical care may indeed be the equivalent of a death sentence. Therefore, health care has been declared a "right," presumably as a corollary of the right to life. A "two class system of care" (such as one which provides public hospitals for those unable to pay for private care) is considered an infringement of "equal" rights. Because of its necessity, health care must not be treated as a commodity.

The doctor-patient relationship has been invested with an aura of the sacred. The physician must always act in the best interest of the patient, maintain his confidences, behave honorably, and take all care that is humanly possible in his treatment. Grubby business considerations seem sacrilegious when the physician "holds your life in his hands." The idea of profits in proportion to misery seems obnoxious.

Let us compare other human endeavors with medicine. The idea that physicians alone create demand for their services, though repeatedly proclaimed with great authority, is patently implausible. Physicians do not appear on television, advertising for patients. They employ secretaries to say: "I'm sorry, but the doctor can't see you for three weeks." In contrast, many products would be without a market if advertising were not allowed. Automobile mechanics, insurance salesmen, and stockbrokers all may take advantage of our fear and ignorance to sell us more of their services than we really need. The most notorious group for creating a need for their own talents must be lawyers in legislatures and regulatory bodies, who invent laws no layman could possibly interpret.

Limited Powers

While doctors do sometimes save lives, their power over life and death is often exaggerated in the public mind. They neither give life, nor vanquish death. Their occasional triumph in the struggle with the Angel of Death is only temporary. A substantial part of the doctor's time is spent treating colds and backache, which are hardly life-threatening, or diseases like terminal cancer or cirrhosis of the liver, in which he may offer comfort but not cure. The need for a given medical service is seldom absolute. Many illnesses can be treated just as well at home as in the hospital; many diagnostic tests are of marginal value; and many treatments improve somewhat the probability of a good outcome, at the price of introducing new risks of harm from the treatment itself.

Not only do doctors have limited weapons against premature death; they are by no means the only providers of the necessities of life. If their services are conscripted with the justification of the right to life, then what about those who produce food and shelter, which are continual, not merely episodic needs? And while the physician has the responsibility of trying to save the sick and injured, how much heavier are the responsibilities of those who can kill people in the best of health, such as engineers who design bridges or power plants, airplane pilots, and mechanics who repair brakes?

Marketable Qualities

Health itself is not a commodity; it cannot be purchased for any amount of money. Things which can be purchased include drugs, diagnostic tests (and the equipment which makes them possible), and the time of people with expertise. Medical devices do not undergo spontaneous generation. Since somebody must invest money in creating them, to say that one person has a right to their use is incompatible with another's right to his property. Medicine is labor intensive. The nurse, the x-ray technician, the electrician, the cook, and the janitor must be paid, or they stop coming to work. Even the doctor must earn a living, and to take in laundry would interfere with the ability to see patients.

Because the doctor intervenes in areas related to the patient's physical and spiritual integrity, and because the patient is often impaired by sickness or anxiety, a violation of trust in the doctor-patient relationship is particularly reprehensible. Nevertheless, the fundamental demands made on the doctor are not unique. Bankers and lawyers must maintain confidences and put the interest of their clients ahead of their own. Professors must refrain from seducing students. Plumbing contractors must give honest estimates and do careful work. Honor is required of men of every calling in their relationships with others.

Medicine is a quasi-priesthood only to the extent that magic is involved. In fact, magic and art remain important ingredients in healing. However, patients rightfully demand science and technical skill in addition, and for these payment has traditionally been expected. (If technology becomes the only aspect of medical care that is well compensated, the science fiction writers may be prophets: In *The Empire Strikes Back,* all the doctors appear to be robots.)

Do doctors really profit from patients' misery? If the doctor deliberately made the patient sick, then the accusation would be just. Bakers don't profit from causing human hunger, but from relieving it. Plumbers don't profit from the existence of human needs for drinking water and waste disposal, but for providing sanitary means for meeting them.

The Profit Motive in Various Practice Arrangements

To condemn the profit motive in medicine is a hook. By logical extension, one must condemn it everywhere. Yet the question is not whether the profit motive will operate in medicine, as in any field of human action, but how, and to whose advantage, it will work. Profits are incentives, and may consist of money, power, prestige, or leisure time. Are incentives in a market economy more likely to benefit the patient than those in a socialized one?

Aren't most hospitals and clinics nonprofit? Or weren't they before the intrusion of big health care corporations? Although many excellent voluntary hospitals exist, their nonprofit status does not exclude big returns to some people affiliated with them. Returns may not be forthrightly called profits. For example, a dapper young man with a degree in social science is planning a health awareness program intended to prevent illness by counseling people about their lifestyle. "It will be nonprofit," he emphasized.

"Oh, how will you make a living?"

"I'll get a salary, of course."

"What's the difference between your salary, and my taking home the profits of my business?"

A benign smile was the only answer. One difference, of course, is that the salary is paid regardless of whether or not there are profits. If income does not exceed expenditures, then let the equipment suppliers, the landlord, and the bank take the loss. Another difference is that he'll be charging more to tell people they are fat and flabby than I ask for a complete history and physical examination. Furthermore, he will not be paying personal property or business license taxes.

Given that doctors must earn a living (albeit not so much money that they must flaunt their conspicuous consumption), why should the patient want to pay him directly for each service, instead of by salary? The fee for service may encourage the doctor to prescribe unnecessary treatments. Unquestionably, some unscrupulous doctors make a lot of money from useless injections.

One reason for payment of extra services is that people are sometimes willing to do for money things they wouldn't do for love. Examples include driving to the emergency room at midnight, listening to patients with endless vague complaints, or looking up a bleeding rectum on Christmas Eve. The tendency to "buff and turf" when confronted with an unpleasant and perhaps futile task is only human nature, especially when shirking is rewarded as well as volunteering.

The importance of the fee as part of the treatment was first recognized by psychiatrists. If the patient hasn't sufficient investment in getting better, he may be evasive about cooperating with treatments such as psychoanalysis, which is demanding and painful. Perhaps the unshakable faith patients have in the encapsulated lake scum found in health food stores or in the bizarre prescriptions of the quack is related to the outrageous price they pay. Free medicines often accumulate, untried, in the cupboard.

The Patient as Employer

The most important advantage to the patient in being responsible for his own bill is that he thereby becomes a customer, the physician's employer. While the physician is assumed to have greater knowledge, the customer ultimately makes the decisions. If not satisfied, he may freely seek advice elsewhere. Although the physician at times may be tempted to accede to harmful requests, to avoid losing business, the challenge to his integrity is no greater than in a different system, where the threat may be a letter to a congressman. Just as an honest contractor may have to say "I won't put the roof on that way because it will leak; either do it my way or find another contractor," the physician can suggest finding another doctor. Both physician and patient are protected when they have freedom of association.

The beneficiaries of public medicine are no longer customers, but consumers. Unable to exert their influence directly with their dollars, they must be represented by a patient advocate. The relationship between patient and physician may in fact be involuntary for one or both parties. The agency dispensing the paycheck intrudes, dividing the physician's loyalty. The consumer may be considered an adversary of the agency if he demands more than his "fair share" of services, while the physician is held responsible for preventing "overutilization." The doctor is the "gatekeeper" to expensive consultations and diagnostic tests. The patient has an investment in assuming a sick role, since more services and attention become available to him without additional charge. In a prepaid arrangement, that's the only way to get his money's worth. If the consumer is displeased, he cannot fire the physician as the customer would, but can complain to the ombudsman, the chief of staff, or his senator. His influence may be negligible, or magnified out of all proportion.

Although many wish that medical care were aloof from the market place, market phenomena invariably occur even as efforts are made to insulate health services from market pressures. As the price barrier is removed, demand skyrockets. Sitting in the waiting room at the local Veterans Administration hospital reminds one of the gasoline lines, and many people withdraw from prepaid health plans because of the lengthy waits. Waiting time seems inversely proportional to the price of goods or services offered. People in queues have a natural angry reaction: They demand some authority who will see that the greedy providers allocate resources more equitably. Somebody must set up a priority system, or print ration tickets.

Subsidized Demand

While complaints arise that medical care is still not adequately available to some, others cry that already we spend too much on it. Few recognize the explanation: People are always less thrifty when spending other people's money than when spending their own. In collectivized payment plans (whether government or insurance plans), some way of controlling expenditures is clearly imperative. Insurance companies have discovered the price of socializing risks while individualizing benefits. Though providing for catastrophes by means of insurance is responsible and rational, even this approach entails moral hazard, in that beneficiaries may try to extract more from the insurance than is justified.

Fire insurance may reward arson, and health insurance may reward disability.[4] To attempt to insure routine expenses compounds the problem. A patient who really doesn't need an X-ray may want one anyway, "just to be sure," because the insurance will pay for it. The patient who says "spare no expense" is seldom planning to pay the bill himself. While our society encourages people to become risk-averse and demand a Cadillac insurance policy, the Chevrolet makes equally good sense in insurance and in transportation. The insurance premiums are a given. If one chooses a minimum policy for disasters, and invests the difference in premiums, with luck one may have a profitable investment. If not so lucky, routine out-of-pocket expenses may still cost less than a deluxe policy.

Cost-Control Mechanisms

Having the customer pay a greater part of the bill is generally not the favored proposal for controlling costs or stimulating competition. Usually some type of prepaid plan is envisioned. Not only are the risks to be socialized, but also the benefits. The availability of services is to be based on cost-benefit analysis. Since society pays, society must benefit. Are pneumococcal vaccines to be covered? Let us calculate the cost incurred by society from x preventable cases of pneumonia. Lowered productivity, expenses for X-rays and antibiotics, and even some deaths will occur. Is this price greater than that of y immunizations? The analysis is much more complicated than the process of saying: "This vaccine reduces your chance of getting pneumococcal pneumonia. Is it worth $15 to you?" The former also multiplies many times the impact of an error in calculation, which must be based on uncertain data.

Some of the cost-control (rationing) mechanisms in prepaid or public health plans are administrative. An algorithm may be devised, directing that a chest X-ray shall be ordered if (and only if) certain indications are present. The physician or other provider, such as a nurse practitioner, may deviate from the recommendations, but will have to justify his action if audited. A "hassle factor" may be introduced. At a Veterans Administration hospital, the signature of the chief of service was required on all requisitions for brain scans, when it was felt that that service was being ordered too often.

If the consumer's incentive to save money has been eliminated, why not invent one for the providers? Many health maintenance organizations have done just that. Instead of paying people for doing tests and performing services, they are paid for *not* doing them. Money that is budgeted but not spent may be divided up among the physicians as a bonus. The profit motive is neatly turned around. Unless we assume that prepaid plans attract only physicians of sterling character, surgeons who previously were tempted to do unnecessary surgery may now be reluctant to do operations from which the patient would benefit.

When entrusting planning and decision-making to a central agency, one assumes that the planners are smarter than individual practitioners and, most importantly, have the right values. Naturally, they may not correspond to the values of certain patients. As one Veterans Administration physician said about "too many" hernia operations: "Let them wear a truss." I have yet to find a patient who preferred that alternative.

All rules and regulations can be circumvented by ingenious people. If Medicare doesn't cover custodial care, the doctor can order an intravenous feeding, and change the category to skilled nursing. Since Medicare doesn't cover housecalls to give enemas or transportation for outpatient diagnostic tests, the patient may elect to be admitted to the hospital for some X-rays. Cost-control devices may ultimately increase costs, as people respond to incentives the planners hadn't recognized.

Should the Doctor Be a Slave, a Keeper, or a Servant?

Collectivism in medicine will undoubtedly change the doctor-patient relationship as well as altering the distribution of services. Such proposals are based on the idea that medical care is a right. The strategy of this hook is to divert attention from the question of the impact on personal liberty, by not mentioning the duty corresponding to the right. Physicians potentially become slaves, with the amorphous public (represented, of course, by an authority) as the slaveholder. Rather more likely is that they will become the keepers, depending upon how much influence they exert on the central planners. An ominous development in the medical literature is the frequent use of the term "noncompliant." More familiar in its use by bureaucrats regarding adherence to regulations, it now refers to patients who don't take their medicine or follow their diet.

The emphasis placed on the importance of lifestyle for health has disturbing implications. Normally, I am not inclined to care about how much my neighbor drinks, smokes, or exercises. But if I'm paying the intensive care bills resulting from his gastrointestinal bleeding, emphysema, or heart attack, my interest in his private life mounts. In Communist China, living a healthful life is considered a patriotic duty. Everyone becomes his brother's jailer, as he is taught to be responsible for the behavior of family and neighbors.

The physician will be the servant of whoever pays him (or risk his livelihood). All contracts are validated by "consideration," which is usually money. The same writers who condemn the avarice of physicians under fee for service ask us to rely on the altruism of physicians under other economic arrangements. As patients decline to provide the consideration, they relinquish their decision-making role, which many agencies are all too ready to take over.

Conclusions

A hook is a condemnation of the status quo, without critical examination of the alternatives. Before dismantling our fee-for-service economy, we should outline our goals and see whether other systems can meet them better.

Is the goal to reduce unnecessary surgery? The rate of tonsillectomies in China is very high, without the incentive of Blue Shield.[5] Do we want to reduce hospital stays? The Mayo Clinic, a totally fee-for-service organization, has succeeded as well as prepaid plans.[6] The average length of stay is 15 days in the Soviet Union, compared with five in the United States.[7] Do we wish to distribute expensive equipment fairly? The regional planners put the CT scanner, the *cause célèbre* for cost containment, at St. Luke's Hospital rather than at Harlem, where head trauma victims are more commonly seen. As a result, in a single year only 14 percent of the 1,870 patients for whom the test was recommended actually received it under a "sharing" arrangement.[8] Are we concerned about reducing fear? Patients in the Soviet Union do not have to fear the cost of a serious illness—they have prepaid in stifling if unacknowledged taxes. Instead, they fear the indifference of the doctor, the filth in the operating room, and shortages of the most basic drugs and supplies.[9] Are we interested in making medicine responsive to consumer demand? In the Soviet Union, the logical endpoint of the total institutionalization of medicine has been reached:

The Hippocratic Oath is forbidden, because it might interfere with the physician's loyalty to the employer, the state.[10]

"What about the poor?" is the most pervasive, recurrent question of the supporters of socialism. While medicine has a long history of helping the unfortunate, the results are called "inequitable," and the method "patching" or "reformist."[11] Marxists use our duty to help the poor as a hook for undermining the entire economic structure, with no concern for the observable consequences of worsening the plight of the poor and multiplying their number.

Once health benefits are socialized, on the basis that medical care is different from other economic activities, the fundamental similarities will become apparent. To be logically consistent, collectivization must be extended to other enterprises, or undone in medicine. The former course is more probable; turning away from collectivist morality is a phenomenon rarely observed to date. The hook is indeed a fearful weapon.

---

1. James L. Tyson, *Target America* (Chicago: Regnery Gateway, 1981), p. 19.

2. Cotton M. Lindsay, ed., *New Directions in Public Health Care: A Prescription for the 1980s* (San Francisco: Institute for Contemporary Studies, 1980), p. 194.

3. D. S. Brody, "The Patient's Role in Clinical Decision-Making," *Annals of Internal Medicine*, vol. 93, 1980, pp. 718–722.

4. George Gilder, *Wealth and Poverty* (New York: Basic Books, 1981), p. 108.

5. William V. McDermott, "The China Syndrome," *Archives of Surgery*, vol. 116, 1981, pp. 245–246.

6. Fred T. Nobrega, Iqbal Krishan, Robert K. Smoldt, *et al.*, "Hospital Use in a Fee-for-Service System," *Journal of the American Medical Association*, vol. 247, 1982, pp. 805–809.

7. William A. Knaus, *Inside Russian Medicine* (New York: Everest House, 1981), p. 123.

8. John C. M. Brust, P. C. Taylor Dickinson, Edward B. Healton, "Failure of CT Sharing in a Large Municipal Hospital," *New England Journal of Medicine*, vol. 304, 1981, pp. 1388–1393.

9. Knaus, *op. cit.*

10. M. G. Field, *Doctor and Patient in Soviet Russia* (Cambridge, Mass.: Harvard University Press, 1957), p. 174.

11. Howard Waitzkin, "A Marxist View of Medical Care," *Annals of Internal Medicine*, vol. 89, 1978, pp. 264–278.

II. THE HIGH PRICE OF EXPERIENCE

The British Nationalized Health Service

George Winder

The late Lord Horder, who was one of Great Britain's most distinguished surgeons, speaking prior to the time Britain's medical system was taken over by the state, said, "It is universally acknowledged that our health services are the best in the world."

It is probable that a good many other countries will have made the same claim so we shall not press the point except to say that in 1948, when a socialist government established the British National Health Service, it took over a medical system well up to the standards of the time.

Yet that government seems to have been quite certain that once in the control of the state this system would improve. Many socialist Members of Parliament claimed that the country had, in fact, no medical organization, for they could not conceive of such a thing without a central authority to guide it. The central control which they established would, they believed, not only secure a more efficient medical service but would also ensure a cheaper one. The expected cost of the new National Health Service had been carefully worked out beforehand by the famous economist, now Lord Beveridge, who arrived at an estimate of £170 million a year. This was less than the £180 million which all medical services were believed to have cost the people in private expenditure before the war. Moreover, it was claimed that this figure should not have changed much by 1965; the improvement in general health which the nationalized services would bring about should prevent any increased costs.

Britain's National Health Service has now functioned for fourteen years so let us see to what extent the high hopes for it have been fulfilled.

Mr. Winder, a former Solicitor of the Supreme Court of New Zealand and farmer in England, has written widely on law, agriculture, and economics. This article originally appeared in *The Freeman,* August 1962.

The Estimate Was Low

The first and most obvious fact is the gross error in the forecast of costs that was made by Lord Beveridge. In its first year the nationalized service cost not £170 million but £377 million. The figure has risen year by year; in 1960 it cost £820 million, of which only £23 million was for capital expenditure.

The British Cost of Living Index shows that most prices were multiplied by three between 1938 and 1960. Medical costs, however, are more than four and a half times what they were. This, as we shall see later, has been due, not to any increased remuneration going to doctors, but chiefly to increased hospital expenses.

Below are the published costs of three famous hospitals, in 1938 when they were charitable trusts, and in 1960 when they were state institutions.

	Number of beds		Average weekly cost per patient	
Hospital	1938	1960	1938	1960
Guys	690	630	£6/ 3/ 8	£36/10/11
Charing Cross	293	286	£4/10/ 1	£36/14/11
Royal Portsmouth	250	205	£2/ 9/11	£23/ 8/10

These show a rise of costs from six to nine times—far above any increase which can be accounted for by inflation. These figures are typical of an increase which has taken place in all of Britain's hospitals. Administrative costs, included in the above figures, have risen from eleven to eighteen times, although hospitals no longer have to collect funds from many sources as they did under the old system.

The rising costs of drugs and pharmaceutical preparations have also been of concern to the government. In 1950 these were £37 million and in 1960, £89 million. In 1951, in an effort to prevent waste, the government imposed a charge of one shilling on each prescription. This was increased to two shillings in 1961.

Both these charges were hotly resented by the socialists as being departures from their principle of free medicine. As a socialist Member of Parliament once expressed it, "If the Tories laid their sacrilegious hands on the Health Service, which the Opposition regarded as the very temple of the nation's social security system, the Labour Party would fight it with the same determination which they had brought to fighting the Rent Act." Such tirades, however, had no effect on the conservative government in its determination to enforce these minor charges, even though they have not stopped the rise in total cost of drugs and pharmaceutical preparations.

Better Service?

That all British medical services cost so much more in real terms than they did before they were nationalized might be tolerable if the services the people receive had correspondingly increased. But who can value that intimate association which should exist between the patient and his doctor? Under the old system of free enterprise the doctor was an authoritative master, a trusted friend, and at the same time a servant of his patient who must pay his fee. Under the system now practiced in Great Britain, much of this excellent relationship is undoubtedly retained; nevertheless, it is interrupted by an invisible stranger in the form of a higher medical authority peering over the doctor's shoulder with power to criticize his work and inflict a fine upon him if he is too experimental in his treatment or prescribes too many expensive drugs. The doctor is no longer the servant of the patient but of the National Health Service.

The importance of this change in the doctor's status is difficult to measure. The old traditions are still a powerful force with every honest doctor, but there can be no doubt that the former relationship between the doctor and his patient is slowly being undermined; and this tendency will increase as control passes to a younger generation of medical men who have never known the old ways.

There is little doubt that if the matter were put to a vote the British people after fourteen years of experience would still endorse the nationalized system. But this by no means indicates that they are getting better medical services than before; it merely means that they mistakenly believe such services are now costing them nothing.

To the man who is ill, the fact that he can call on a doctor and pay no fee seems to be such an obvious boon that he usually is oblivious to the price he is in fact paying. Thirteen percent of the cost of the

National Health Service is paid in National Insurance Contributions, 4 percent in minor charges, and the rest in general taxation. This supposedly free medical service costs an average of over a pound per week per family. One would have to be very ill to pay more than this in direct fees. It is this lack of association between services rendered and payments made which induces the British voter to turn a blind eye to the defects of his National Health Service.

The Function of Price

As everyone knows, the strength of a demand for any service very largely depends upon its price. When the state took over Britain's medical services and announced that in the future they were to be free, there was an instant and unprecedented increase in the demand for them. Under free enterprise whenever there is a great increase in the demand for any service there is almost always a consequent increase in its supply. Does the same principle apply to socialized medicine? At first glance, yes. In 1952 there were 27,879 doctors employed by the National Health Service either in hospitals or as general medical practitioners. The number had increased by 1960 to 32,223. The greater increase took place in the hospitals where the number of salaried doctors rose from 9,650 in 1950 to 12,300 in 1960, that is, by 27 percent. During the same period, however, the number of staffed hospital beds increased only $4^{1}/_{2}$ percent, from 453,000 to 473,000. This can be contrasted with a 33 percent increase between 1929 and 1938 under the competitive system. In 1935 there were more hospital beds in Britain per thousand inhabitants than there are today, yet one of the chief charges made by the socialists against the competitive system was that it had insufficient hospital beds. The small increase in the number of beds, together with the fact that there were 466,000 people on the waiting list for such beds in 1960, certainly suggests that the National Health Service has failed to meet the increased demand that the absence of medical fees has made upon it. This great shortage of beds has caused the authorities to institute a system of priorities. Acute cases can always be found a bed, but those requiring operations for such complaints as hernia, varicose veins, and the like may have to wait up to a year and longer.

Perhaps the chief reason for this failure of the National Health Service is that since its inception the building of hospitals has almost ceased. Only one hospital was built in thirteen years. Many socialist doctors before nationalization believed that when the government took over, all financial worries would disappear. With unlimited funds, the government would hasten to build all the hospitals required. In practice the position has been exactly the opposite. The government has been far more cautious in its capital expenditure than the most conservative of private concerns. Overwhelmed by the unexpected and ever-increasing cost of its Health Service, it has tried to keep down expenditure by checking expansion.

Mr. D. S. Lees, a Senior Lecturer in Economics, in an excellent booklet, "Health Through Choice," has pointed out that this failure to spend money on new hospitals has been an outstanding feature of the British nationalized Health Service. Whereas before the war the yearly expenditure for capital purposes was about 20 percent of current health expenditure, since nationalization it has been only about 5 percent. Many medical men believe that nationalization has actually retarded the development of Britain's medical services and that the British people are receiving a far poorer service than they would have received if the prewar system had been allowed to continue its development.

In "The Genesis of the British National Health Service," written by the well known economist John Jewkes and his wife, the authors support the above conclusion, pointing out that in 1939 Great Britain was more amply supplied with hospital beds in proportion to population than the United States, but that since the war this advantage has disappeared. "It is difficult to escape the conclusion that in the United States the quantity of medical services available for each person is larger and is tending to increase more rapidly than in Great Britain."

They also make comparisons with the medical services of Switzerland which for the most part are still under the competitive system. The Swiss have more doctors and many more hospital beds per 1,000 of population. Between 1948 and 1959, money spent on hospital building per head of population was four times as great in Switzerland as in comparatively wealthy Great Britain. Waiting lists in Swiss hospitals are literally unknown.

True, the British government at last has been stung into activity by constant criticism and this year commended a program to spend £50 million building hospitals over the next five years. Whether this expenditure will eliminate the long waiting lists for hospital beds remains to be seen.

These waiting lists have angered the socialists who seem to have forgotten that they are responsible for the introduction of the nationalized hospital. In their publicity at the General Election in 1959 they stated, "Nearly half a million people are waiting for hospital beds; too many doctors' surgeries are still grim and gloomy; too many hospitals are still out-of-date and makeshift; the mental hospitals are overcrowded and dilapidated and, in spite of gallant efforts by those in charge, are quite unsuitable for modern psychiatric care; the committees and staff of the Service have been frustrated by endless administrative delays, and inevitably enthusiasm has been diminished."

No Evidence of Progress

As for the hopeful claim made by Lord Beveridge that the Health Service would improve the health of the people, there is no evidence whatever of this. Infant mortality rates have improved, but so have they in many other countries with entirely different medical systems. Tuberculosis, pneumonia, and diphtheria have diminished, but the same is true elsewhere. Chronic diseases, cancer, and neurosis have increased.

It was claimed that the expenditure on the National Health Service was a form of national investment which would increase wealth by reducing the amount of days lost to industry through sickness; but figures for absence from work on account of illness have in no way diminished.

In summation, the British National Health Service has failed to meet the increased demands made upon it, and even after the change in the value of money is allowed for, medical attention costs the British people a great deal more than before the war. Moreover, in those material factors which lend themselves to measurement, Britain's medical services have expanded far more slowly than they did in the 30 years before nationalization. They also have expanded more slowly than in the United States and Switzerland where medical treatment has remained, for the most part, on a free enterprise basis. If the British people still believe in their state-owned National Health Service, it is not because of its virtues but solely because of the illusion that it costs them nothing.

What the Poor Had to Lose

It may be argued that at least the poor have benefited by not having to pay the doctor's fees. Even this is doubtful. Prior to nationalization, the great amount of charitable hospital service, which then existed, looked after them. Today, the poor must share with others the crowded surgeries which are the result of "free medicine."

It could be argued, of course, that these crowded surgeries and hospitals are evidence of the crying need for a free medical service which must have existed before nationalization but was concealed by the inability of the poor to pay the doctor's fees. But the crowded surgeries are not due so much to seriously sick people asking for treatment they could not previously afford as to the desire of many people to have free treatment for the slightest cold or illness. Before nationalization, a seriously sick person was sure of treatment whatever his financial means. Now, with the many claims on the doctors' services, a sick person may fail to get the attention his illness requires.

If we look upon the National Health Service as a form of charity, it is worth considering whether the British people really need it. Whereas in 1960 health services cost them £820 million, their beer and spirits cost £1,001 million and their tobacco £1,140 million.

It is sometimes claimed that the chief beneficiaries of the nationalized system are the middle classes who, prior to the National Health Service, had to pay their doctor's fees. It is difficult to see their gain, however. The taxes they pay for medical services they may not receive average well over a pound a week per family. The middle classes do, in fact, pay for medical care, the only real difference being that now they are deprived of some of that personal responsibility which was once the basis of their character.

Only about five percent of the people now employ those doctors who have kept out of the National Health Service. They pay twice over, for they must also pay in taxation their share of costs for the nationalized service.

An Ambiguous Position

In considering the doctor himself under Britain's National Health Service, the word "nationalized" may seem a bit out of order. The position of the general practitioner, for instance, is an ambiguous one. He may still have his own private patients if he can get them; but the doctor who originally believed he could get the best of both worlds by having both paying and state patients soon found that the vast majority of them preferred to register under the state system, thus retaining his services at no apparent cost to themselves. The result is that all but a few British doctors now depend on the National Health Service for a living.

Some 600 doctors remained outside the scheme from the beginning and are allowed to carry on under the old competitive system. Lately, these independent practitioners have grown in number, probably due to the growth in private health insurance. In 1948 some 100,000 people subscribed to private health policies; in 1960 more than 1,000,000. According to Dr. John Hunt, secretary of the College of General Practitioners, one-quarter of British doctors have insured their families for private hospital treatment.

The general practitioners employed by the National Health Service are paid, not according to the amount of work they do or the number of patient they attend, but according to the number they can persuade to register on their panel for medical services if they should be required. For every patient on his panel, a doctor receives a fee, whether he attends such patient or not. Therefore, the majority of general practitioners aim to get as many registered patients as possible. A doctor is expected to accept on his panel everyone who applies. But he naturally does his best to avoid potential patients who might require his services too often, such as old people and chronic invalids.

A general practitioner is allowed to have up to 3,500 registered patients, yet doctors claim that about 1,500 is all they can properly attend. More than half of Britain's general practitioners have more than 2,500 patients while 29 percent have more than 3,000. For each patient on his panel, a doctor now receives 19/6 ($2.73) a year—occasionally more, to induce a doctor to go into unpopular areas or to a country area where the panel must necessarily be small. There are also allowances for "good behavior" such as attending refresher courses. Out of his capitation fee the doctor must pay the costs of his surgery and the wages of his receptionist or nurse. The fee is the same for the doctor who employs capable assistants and uses the most modern equipment as for the doctor who gets along with the aid of a stethoscope and an overworked wife. The result is that the doctor who accepts only as many patients as he can conscientiously handle will have a very inadequate income. For more income, a doctor must have a large panel of patients, which will mean a crowded surgery, hurried interviews, and often a snap diagnosis. The system places a premium on bad and hasty service. Moreover, because the patient has nothing to pay, he tends to visit his overworked doctor as often as possible. As one doctor has put it, "The patient seeks the doctor to gratify his every whim; the doctor tries everything in his power to avoid the patient."

Under such conditions, it is not surprising when a doctor develops a feeling of guilt and resigns the service, explaining as one did recently, "The horror of this system is that many excellent doctors are trapped by it, but I have hated myself for it and now I am out of it."

Many of the patients also are unhappy. Knowing the reluctance of the doctor to visit them, the more considerate do their best to visit his surgery, though they should have remained in bed. Knowing also that their visit brings the doctor no financial return, some are constantly apologetic. "I'm sorry to trouble you, Doctor," is a phrase constantly on their lips. Others, of course, aggressively insist on their rights and expect the doctor to do anything they demand, such as writing a prescription for some patent medicine they have seen advertised so they can have it at the expense of the National Health Service. Young doctors sometimes are suspected of prescribing too generously in order to attract new patients to their panels. Many doctors believe their surgeries are looked upon as social centers by women patients.

Passing the Buck

There is a minimum service which the doctor feels compelled to perform, but only the more conscientious will go beyond this. Most, if they can possibly do so, send their more troublesome jobs to the hospitals, thus adding to the already excessive demands upon those institutions. Simple operations, formerly taken in stride, are now handled this way, as are such time-consuming jobs as a check-up to find out the patient's general state of health. The District Medical Executive

Councils do not seem to resent this passing of responsibility to the crowded hospitals. They even encourage it by forbidding the general practitioner to do a number of jobs which were formerly within his province. In most areas, he is not allowed to do X-rays or blood tests or perform regularly on women patients the cancer-warning Papanicolous test.

One of the most constant complaints of the general practitioner is the great amount of paperwork required by the authorities. The majority of British doctors may still have the skills and loyalties inherited from the past, but under the National Health Service they have every reason to forget them and to take as little responsibility as possible. Whatever service they may render their patients will not in any way affect their capitation fee.

Since nationalization, the people have developed a habit of suing their doctors in the Law Courts for negligence. Although such actions existed in the past, they have now become much more common. This again makes the general practitioner reluctant to do more than the minimum required of him. After all, there is a limit to the responsibility one can undertake for 19 shillings and 6 pence. Moreover, medical colleagues on the salaried hospital staff are in no such invidious position, for the government is responsible for their mistakes. This has caused some doctors to suggest that the general medical practitioner would be better off as a salaried official than he is under the present system, in which he has all the disadvantages but none of the advantages of independence.

It is worth noting that this British system of socialized medicine with its capitation payments was adopted in Australia in 1946 by a socialist government. In 1952 a conservative government abolished it, replacing it by insurance against illness through private companies. Although the government did not entirely desert the medical field, it restored the old and well-tried relationship between doctor and patient. This government, incidentally, is still in power.

Third-Party Medicine

In the past the doctor was responsible only to his patient and to public opinion. Now he has a higher authority which he must conciliate. He may be told, for example, by his District Medical Executive Council that he is giving his patient too many drugs of an expensive kind and that his drug bill which the state has to meet is above the average for his district. If these excessive costs are continued, he may be required to pay a proportion of the bill himself. Here is a paradoxical instruction to doctors from a recent memorandum by the Ministry of Health: "Without prejudice to the doctor's rights to prescribe whatever he thinks necessary in any individual case, a doctor may be called upon to justify the cost of his prescription." Another memorandum, evidently trying to overcome the natural reluctance of the panel doctor to visit the patient, gives full instruction as to when such visits should be made.

Another cross the general practitioner must bear is that a patient may inform the District Medical Executive Council that his doctor is not giving him the full service to which he feels entitled. Occasionally the public is regaled in the press with a list of fines inflicted on doctors who have committed such offenses as failing to answer night calls. In 1960, disciplinary action was taken against doctors in 410 cases.

But what most troubles the general medical practitioner is that his fixed fee, multiplied by more patients than he can adequately serve, leaves him with a far lower real income than most doctors enjoyed before the war.

Doctors Are Leaving

In 1951, after an inquiry on the remuneration of doctors, the capitation rate and the salaries of hospital doctors were raised to compensate for inflation. Since then, rates have risen only slightly, but prices generally are up a third, causing a decline in the real income of doctors. Naturally, doctors are dissatisfied. Older members of the profession seldom can do anything about it, but the younger members are showing their disapproval by simply leaving the country. John R. Seale, M.D., M.R.C.P., has shown the extent of this exodus in a booklet published by The Fellowship for Freedom in Medicine. Although doctors have always emigrated from Great Britain, they are leaving now at a rate higher than ever before. Between 1956 and 1960, of doctors trained in British medical schools, 1,070 have emigrated to Canada, 1,100 to Australia, 190 to New Zealand, and 750 to the U.S. In the twelve months of 1960 more doctors trained in England and Ireland emigrated to the U.S. than in the whole period from 1930 to 1939. Canadian statistics show that British doctors are entering Canada at a rate five times as great as that for British immigrants in general. Last year, one-third of the medical students who qualified in Great Britain left the country.

Moreover, knowledge of the disadvantages under which British doctors are now serving has penetrated to the rising generation. Although the number of students at British universities has doubled since the war, the number studying medicine has actually decreased since the introduction of the National Health Service. There were 14,200 medical students at British universities in 1950 compared with 12,700 in 1958. The resulting vacuum in the British Health Service has to be filled with doctors from the Commonwealth and by foreigners. Before the war, some 200 Commonwealth doctors a year registered in Great Britain, chiefly from Canada, Australia, and New Zealand. In 1960 the number was 1,400, mostly from India and Pakistan. The number of foreign doctors registering before the war with the British Medical Council was under a dozen a year. In 1960 it was 1,701 and last year over 2,000—from such places as Syria, Spain, Greece, Peru, Turkey, Japan, and Yugoslavia. Some of these are well trained, but as Dr. Seale points out, others are from medical schools of which the British authorities can have very little knowledge. Nearly half of all junior posts are now held by doctors from overseas.

A report issued by the Nuffield Provincial Trust showed that in many casualty departments the provision of medically qualified supervision had broken down and that able nursing sisters were making the diagnosis and carrying out the treatment. A doctor was usually available, but often he spoke no language in which he could be understood. Recently the General Hospital at Weston-super-Mare advertised for a Senior House Officer in Surgery. It received applications from one Briton, one Australian, one Portuguese, one Greek, one Japanese, three Anglo-Indians, three Egyptians, five Pakistanis, and forty-three Indians.

Young British doctors who have some memory and regard for older medical traditions seem to be expressing their opinion of their National Health Service in that manner sometimes described as "voting with their feet." British nurses are infected by the same spirit. There is a general dissatisfaction with their rates of pay and, for the first time in British history, there has been talk of a nurses' strike. Fortunately, the high ideals of the profession have prevailed. It takes some time to undermine a good medical system and particularly to destroy the long-established traditions of trust between doctor and patient which the older British doctors remember. Nevertheless, the British National Health Service is doing both.

Perhaps the greatest tragedy is that the generation of Britons now growing to manhood may unquestioningly accept the National Health Service, for they never will have known anything better.

The British Way of Withholding Care

by Harry Schwartz

The problems associated with socialized medicine can be symbol-ized by the fate of two children, David Barber and Matthew Collier, who died in early 1988 in the British city of Birmingham.

Both children needed heart transplants to survive. Their parents became so desperate that they sued Britain's National Health Service to force the NHS to provide the necessary medical care. Their efforts were in vain: Neither child got the operation, and neither child is alive today.

The point is not that those who run socialized health-care systems would rather see children die than give them the care they need to survive. Rather, the point is that all socialized systems lack one thing: enough money to provide quality medical care and to take full advantage of modern medical technology.

In other words, the propagandists are stretching the truth a long way when they insist that socialized medicine provides a bountiful distribution of all the medical care people could want or need. In reality, medical care is rationed in socialized systems. Managers must decide which patients will be sacrificed because the total amount of care provided is based on the total amount of money available.

J. Enoch Powell, a former British cabinet member who ran the NHS for three years, summed up the situation when he said that the demand for free medical care is infinite and cannot be satisfied by a country's limited resources. David Barber and Matthew Collier are two depressing examples of what can happen when the demand for care outstrips the supply of money.

Britain is not the only country plagued by the pitfalls of socialized medicine. Until recently, the Soviet Union's medical system was

Dr. Schwartz lives in Scarsdale, New York. This article, a reprint of his May 1988 column in *Private Practice* magazine, appeared in the March 1989 *Freeman*.

praised to the skies by Soviet propaganda and by naive Americans who were taken in by that propaganda.

But now that the current Soviet ruler, Mikhail S. Gorbachev, has called for open and honest discussion of his country's problems, the truth has emerged: Russia's health-care system is—and has long been—a disaster. Basic medicines are in short supply, while equipment to treat serious illnesses such as kidney disease is virtually unavailable.

For instance, the Soviet media have revealed that the country's infant-mortality rate in recent years has been two-and-a-half to three times greater than that of the United States. The death rate for all Soviet citizens actually is rising, and many hospitals lack even basic supplies and equipment. These revelations explain why, for most of the past two decades, the Soviet Union hasn't bothered to report statistics on its infant mortality and death rates.

As more and more of American medicine is socialized through the Medicare program for senior citizens and the Medicaid program for the poor, rationing—the denial of care to save money for the government—is becoming evident here, too.

For example, in Oregon, legislators recently decided that the state would not finance heart and liver transplants. Instead, they made more money available for preventive activities such as prenatal care. As a result, a number of Oregon citizens whose lives could have been saved by transplants were told, in effect, to go ahead and die because the Oregon Medicaid program would not help them.

Diagnosis Related Groups

The chief method of rationing care in the Medicare program is the system of diagnosis related groups, under which hospitals are paid a fixed amount to treat beneficiaries. The reimbursements are based on each patient's initial diagnosis. As a result, hospitals try to discharge senior citizens as quickly as possibly because the less time they stay in the hospital, the more profit the hospital makes.

Medicare managers already are trying to introduce a much more radical method of rationing health care by getting as many senior citizens as they can to enroll in health maintenance organizations.

If this effort to boost HMO enrollment is successful, the government will save money because HMOs will receive a fixed amount annually for each member, regardless of how much medical care that member receives. This means that HMOs have an incentive to give as little care as possible. The less care provided, the more money HMOs will make.

One or two generations ago, many people dreamed that socialized medicine would provide every citizen with all the health care he needed or wanted. But history has proved irrefutably that socialized medicine is simply a means of imposing Procrustean rationing on the entire population. In other words, some citizens receive care and live, while others are denied care and are permitted to die as quickly as possible.

Why I Left England

by Edward L. McNeil, M.D.

I am often asked why I left England and the National Health Service to come to this country. There is no simple answer like "money," "opportunity," "politics," or "climate," but if I describe the conditions under which I found myself practicing medicine in England, the reader may find his own answers.

When I qualified as a physician and surgeon, the NHS had been established for five years and there was virtually no private practice of medicine in England. The practice of medicine in wartime did not offer any relevant basis for comparison with the system I found myself involved in; nor did the practice of medicine before 1939 as, in retrospect, that was another era about which the older practitioners were reluctant to talk. (I naturally suspected the old system of private practice wasn't good.)

My only knowledge of private practice in the U.S.A. was from a small number of patients and friends who had been there and reported that medical care was very expensive and that one had to establish credit at a hospital before being treated or admitted.

It was not until I had been in my own solo practice in Yonkers, New York, for about two years that I realized the tremendous advantages of the private practice system.

As a student I had always been more inclined toward the surgical disciplines, so my first "house job" was as House Surgeon in a London hospital with two surgical wards, 36 male beds, and 36 female beds. There was also a smaller ward of about 10 beds which was used to isolate clean orthopedic cases and serve as a spare ward for overflows of one or the other sex. There was rarely an empty bed, and I had the

---

Dr. McNeil established a private medical practice in the United States in the late 1950s. An innovator in the fields of space medicine and emergency medical care, he is now retired.

This article was reprinted by permission from the January 1971 issue of *Private Practice*, and appeared in the May 1971 *Freeman*.

unpleasant task of turning down at least two out of three requests by GP's for emergency admissions. Selective surgery cases had their admissions arranged through the waiting lists compiled by OPD clinics.

I later learned what it was like to be a GP trying to have a patient admitted for an emergency condition, telephoning five or six different hospitals without success, then, in frustration, sending the patient to the emergency department of a hospital that had already turned down a request for admission, and hoping for the best. In later years, London had what was called the Emergency Bed Service [EBS] to which a GP could direct his requests for admission and they would call all the hospitals for him, then force the hospital they considered most able to adapt to an extra admission to take the patient. (This system was fine in theory, but in practice it would often take the EBS six to twelve hours to find a bed, and some patients could not wait that long.)

As the only house surgeon for at least 80 surgical patients, including some in the pediatric ward, I worked very hard but appreciated the technical experience which I crammed into six months. Within two months of qualifying, I was performing laparotomies in the middle of the night, relying entirely on my own diagnostic abilities, relying on the house physician or obstetric house surgeon (also newly qualified) to give the anesthetic, and relying on only one scrub nurse for my surgical assistance. (Before 5 p.m. I did have an Indian surgical registrar—a senior resident who was an excellent surgical tutor—to guide me, and the two attending surgeons did "rounds" every other day and a rushed "round" after their operating sessions.)

Clinic vs. GP

What humility I had as a "new boy" receded very quickly with the volume of experience, and I soon found myself agreeing with the other house staff that those doctors out there in GP land had minimal medical knowledge and no manners. Fancy an experienced GP sending a patient to the Casualty Department with a scribbled note saying, "Please see and treat," with no history noted or any attempt at diagnosis; and such bad manners, when I had already told him on the telephone that I didn't have any empty beds and we had seven extra beds up in the corridors and down the middle of the ward!

Assisting the Chief and the Registrar at the surgical clinic also put me in the position of advising GP's with decades of experience about the diagnosis and management of their patients. The conceit of youth! At the clinics, the Chief would see the least number of patients and those most potentially interesting. The Registrar would share the remainder with the house surgeon. From the patients' point of view, it was pot luck whether they saw a real surgeon or me.

(Only a few years later, I found myself as a GP referring cases to the clinic and waiting a few months for a letter from a newly qualified pipsqueak house surgeon telling me that the diagnosis had been considered to be "so and so," "such and such" had been done, and the patient was referred back to me on "such and such" medication.)

I quite naturally came to the opinion that a newly qualified physician was at the peak of medical knowledge and know-how and thereafter it was a steady decline in his knowledge and ability. I took comfort in the excellence of my medical training but was repeatedly surprised at meeting situations I had not been taught about and finding patients didn't all respond to treatment as they should. Something seemed wrong with the system.

Little Prospect for Advancement as a Surgeon

As previously mentioned, I was surgically inclined and considered I would eventually become a surgeon. A look at the prospects of surgical colleagues who were five or six years ahead of me in the race made me realize I might as well forget it. I knew many who had spent over five years in the specialty only to quit and go into general practice because the chances of becoming an attending surgeon (known as a Consultant) were so slim. A hospital of over 200 beds would have only one or two surgeons of consultant status and often the same surgeons would cover other hospitals as well. The only vacancies for consultantship occurred when a surgeon died or retired at the age of 65.

The situation in 1956 was that for every vacancy there would be about 70 applications for the post, each applicant having had considerable experience in surgery, holding an FRCS and many also having a Masters Degree in Surgery. Many of the vacancies would be in localities one wouldn't rationally choose as a place to live and bring up a family.

(I have heard that the situation has altered over the last few years and the competition for the posts is not as frustrating. This is because so many of the trained surgeons have emigrated. For many years, over 500 doctors were leaving the United Kingdom each year. Last year approximately 400 left.)

After my first surgical job, I became the house physician in the lovely Wiltshire market town of Salisbury near to Stonehenge. I enjoyed the experience and the six days off I received in the six months. One of the doctors in the hospital had just returned from a residency in the U.S.A., and from him I caught a glimmer that there were other ways to practice hospital medicine—and combine it with general practice.

However, my roots were in England and in its system, and one year of experience was not enough to say it didn't suit me. I entered general practice in a working-class suburb of London in close proximity to where I had been the house surgeon. It did not take me long to question the attitudes and infallibility of the hospital-based doctors when I was wearing the GP's shoes. If I visited my patients who had been admitted to hospital on my old wards, I found I was less than welcome. Other GP's informed me that I would be considered to be interfering if I did visit them.

To supplement my income and get my foot in the door of a hospital, I obtained a post as clinical assistant in the OPD of the Royal National Throat, Nose, and Ear Hospital in London. There, at least, I was able to order some follow-up studies and see some X-rays.

One of my duties in the ENT clinic was to help re-evaluate those children on the waiting list to have their tonsils removed, to see if they should be moved up the list or onto the list with less priority. Some had been on the list six years! (At the time I left, the theoretical waiting time on the day the child's name went on the list was 10 years. This reckoning was with the assumption there would be no modification of priorities, no child would leave the area, and no tonsils would recover without surgery.)

Make the Patient Wait

An ex-Minister of Health, The Right Honorable J. Enoch Powell, admitted in his book *Medicine and Politics,* that the only effective method for putting a brake on the unlimited demand for medical services was making patients wait for services. Many elective surgical procedures such as cholecystectomy and herniorrhaphy have a waiting list for admission. One to two years is not an uncommon time to wait for these procedures. The "novel" method of using "payment for services"—be it only a small price—has been little used as a brake on unlimited demand for services.

Some years ago, when prescription costs were soaring and the NHS was under a greater financial strain than usual, a token charge of approximately 25 cents was placed on each prescription instead of the medication being "free." During the six months following the initiation of this charge, the number of prescriptions decreased by almost 30 percent. With an election in the offing, the government in power at the time interpreted this decrease as meaning that 30 percent of the patients receiving a prescription from a doctor could not afford 25 cents (the cost of one-third of a packet of cigarettes)! The charge was then discontinued.

Much Hard Work—Often Wholly Unnecessary

To return to the subject of my year in general practice, I was already used to working hard and long so the volume of patients seen in the office and on house calls didn't bother me too much until I realized that at least one-quarter of the patients needn't have come to see me at all on the occasion on which they did. The patient load fluctuated too closely with the midweek soccer games being played at home and with the preholiday seasons.

Certificates for sickness absence (after the fact) were always tricky and frequent. If I hinted that I suspected some hanky-panky, the patient usually stuck to the story that he had come to my office but there were too many patients waiting and he felt too sick to sit there and wait. I usually handled the situation by giving the patient the certificate and saying, "Of course, I'm sure YOU were sick but some people use my certificates improperly and they may get me into lots of trouble."

Not having any X-ray facilities in the office, less than meager lab equipment, and little or no time for work-up tests, any patient seen who needed those tests had to be referred to the hospital clinics. A very few simple tests could be referred directly to the hospital lab (mainly those concerned with the diagnosis and treatment of tuberculosis) but anything approaching a blood chemistry, an EKG, or an X-ray could not be ordered by the GP directly, so the patient had to be referred to the appropriate clinic for those doctors running the clinic to decide on the tests and order them.

The result of this angle of the system, plus the difficulty of obtaining a hospital bed for acute conditions such as myocardial infarction, pneumonia, and stroke (especially stroke), meant that a GP treated many of these conditions in the patient's home without any of the ancillary diagnostic aids which would be routine in a hospital. I recognized the satisfaction of "curing" a condition with minimal help of diagnostic equipment and lab tests but there was always that sneaking suspicion at the back of my mind that the patient may not have had the condition I thought I had cured. Without this confirming knowledge, there was no testing of one's diagnostic and therapeutic ability and so improving one's effectiveness as a physician. With my present knowledge of cardiac arrhythmias which can be prevented or ameliorated by information only to be gained from ancillary equipment, I shudder at the risks the patients ran under my care.

Toward the end of my year in general practice it became clear to me that if I remained a GP under the NHS, I would be practicing medicine at an unsatisfactory level both from the point of view of my own lack of opportunities to improve my abilities, and from the point of view of my patients, as there seemed few ways of improving the quality of medical care being given. The urge to see the practice of medicine on the other side of the Atlantic increased so that when the sub-dean of my medical school asked me if I would be interested in a surgical residency in New York, I was on the boat in less than a month.

A Second Look

After a year in New York which opened my eyes to the tremendous opportunities here and the advantages of private practice, I returned to England for a time to clear up personal matters and to see if I had been mistaken about the NHS. I spent a year as Casualty Surgeon in a North Devon hospital in a charming small town from which part of the English fleet sailed to meet the Spanish Armada. My pay ($45 a week) was three times as much as when I was a house surgeon and I was given a nicely furnished apartment, but the bureaucratic administration of the hospital was irksome and wasteful.

The GP's in the area had decided advantages over those in the metropolis and other big cities, insofar as they held appointments as surgeons, internists, and anesthetists on the hospital staff. However, as these men retired or died their posts were filled with full-time specialists, so the future as regards becoming an attending surgeon or a GP with hospital privileges was the same as elsewhere in the country.

Although the hospital was small (fewer than 200 beds) there was a veritable army of administrative assistants. Before nationalization, there had been a maintenance employee who looked after the heating system, lighting, and mechanical appliances, with occasional help from outside private firms. At the time I was there, they had a chief plumber, electrician, heating engineer, and other specialists, all under a chief maintenance officer, all complete with offices, desks, and secretaries, and inventory clerk. The hospital secretary also had a secretary. A few miles away was the governing hospital of the area, with a large administrative staff to pass on orders to the hospitals in the group; and, of course, *they* were passing on orders from the Ministry of Health in London.

The town badly needed a new hospital with a modern building, and the chance of one being built was nil. Since the inception of the NHS in 1948, only three new hospitals have been completed in the whole country. I would be surprised if there were any *counties* in the U.S.A. that have not had at least one new hospital since 1948.

Within two years of returning to this country, I was in private practice and on the staff of three hospitals, and enjoying the immense amount of post-graduate education available in those hospitals. My office was equipped in a manner that would have been only a dream in England. The advantages of having a lab, X-ray equipment, physiotherapy equipment, an EKG machine, and an examining table that was designed to allow proper posturing of the patient were great luxuries to me. They allowed me to offer services to my patients that, to obtain under the NHS, they would have had to shuffle from clinic to clinic and hospital to hospital, hardly ever knowing who the doctor was who examined them.

I have been here permanently for 13 years now and I often wonder what sort of a physician I would be now if I had remained in England. A few years ago, my old medical school sent a list of all the old students. Reading down this list and noting their present addresses, I counted that more than half of those who graduated in my class had left England or the practice of medicine. Others must have thought as I did.

Socialized Medicine: The Canadian Experience

by Pierre Lemieux

The Canadian public health system is often put forward as an ideal for Americans to emulate. It provides all Canadians with free basic health care: free doctors visits, free hospital ward care, free surgery, free drugs and medicine while in the hospital—plus some free dental care for children as well as free prescription drugs and other services for the over-65 and welfare recipients. You just show your plastic medicare card and you never see a medical bill.

This extensive national health system was begun in the late 1950s with a system of publicly funded hospital insurance, and completed in the late 1960s and early 1970s when comprehensive health insurance was put into place. The federal government finances about 40 percent of the costs, provided the provinces set up a system satisfying federal norms. All provincial systems thus are very similar, and the Quebec case which we will examine is fairly typical.

One immediate problem with public health care is with the funding. Those usually attracted to such a "free" system are the poor and the sick—those least able to pay. A political solution is to force everybody to enroll in the system, which amounts to redistributing income toward participants with higher health risks or lower income. This is why the Canadian system is universal and compulsory.

Even if participation is compulsory in the sense that everyone has to pay a health insurance premium (through general or specific taxes), some individuals are willing to pay a second time to purchase private insurance and obtain private care. If you want to avoid this double system, you do as in Canada: You legislate a monopoly for the public health insurance system.

This means that although complementary insurance (providing private or semi-private hospital rooms, ambulance services, etc.) is

---

Mr. Lemieux is an economist and author in Quebec. This article is reprinted from the March 1989 issue of *The Freeman*.

available on the market, sale of private insurance covering the basic insured services is forbidden by law. Even if a Canadian wants to purchase basic private insurance besides the public coverage, he cannot find a private company legally allowed to satisfy his demand.

In this respect, the Canadian system is more socialized than in many other countries. In the United Kingdom, for instance, one can buy private health insurance even if government insurance is compulsory.

In Canada, then, health care is basically a socialized industry. In the Province of Quebec, 79 percent of health expenditures are public. Private health expenditures go mainly for medicines, private or semi-private hospital rooms, and dental services. The question is: How does such a system perform?

The Costs of Free Care

The first thing to realize is that free public medicine isn't really free. What the consumer doesn't pay, the taxpayer does, and with a vengeance. Public health expenditures in Quebec amount to 29 percent of the provincial government budget. One-fifth of the revenues comes from a wage tax of 3.22 percent charged to employers and the rest comes from general taxes at the provincial and federal levels. It costs $1,200 per year in taxes for each Quebec citizen to have access to the public health system. This means that the average two-child family pays close to $5,000 per year for public health insurance. This is much more expensive than the most comprehensive private health insurance plan.

Although participating doctors may not charge more than the rates reimbursed directly to them by the government, theoretically they may opt out of the system. But because private insurance for basic medical needs isn't available, there are few customers, and less than one percent of Quebec doctors work outside the public health system. The drafting of virtually all doctors into the public system is the first major consequence of legally forbidding private insurers from competing with public health insurance.

The second consequence is that a real private hospital industry cannot develop. Without insurance coverage, hospital care costs too much for most people. In Quebec, there is only one private for-profit hospital (an old survivor from the time when the government would issue a permit to that kind of institution), but it has to work within the public health insurance system and with government-allocated budgets.

The monopoly of basic health insurance has led to a single, homogeneous public system of health care delivery. In such a public monopoly, bureaucratic uniformity and lack of entrepreneurship add to the costs. The system is slow to adjust to changing demands and new technologies. For instance, day clinics and home care are underdeveloped as there exist basically only two types of general hospitals: the nonprofit local hospital and the university hospital.

When Prices Are Zero

Aside from the problems inherent in all monopolies, the fact that health services are free leads to familiar economic consequences. Basic economics tells us that if a commodity is offered at zero price, demand will increase, supply will drop, and a shortage will develop.

During the first four years of hospitalization insurance in Quebec, government expenditures on this program doubled. Since the introduction of comprehensive public health insurance in 1970, public expenditures for medical services per capita have grown at an annual rate of 9.4 percent. According to one study, 60 percent of this increase represented a real increase in consumption.[1]

There has been much talk of people abusing the system, such as using hospitals as nursing homes. But then, on what basis can we talk of abusing something that carries no price?

As demand rises and expensive technology is introduced, health costs soar. But with taxes already at a breaking point, government has little recourse but to try to hold down costs. In Quebec, hospitals have been facing budget cuts both in operating expenses and in capital expenditures. Hospital equipment is often outdated, and the number of general hospital beds dropped by 21 percent from 1972 to 1980.

Since labor is the main component of health costs, incomes of health workers and professionals have been brought under tight government controls. In Quebec, professional fees and target incomes are negotiated between doctors' associations and the Department of Health and Social Services. Although in theory most doctors still are independent professionals, the government has put a ceiling on certain categories of income: for instance, any fees earned by a general practitioner in excess of $164,108 (Canadian) a year are reimbursed at a rate of only 25 percent.

Not surprisingly, income controls have had a negative impact on work incentives. From 1972 to 1978, for instance, general practitioners reduced by 11 percent the average time they spent with their patients. In 1977, the first year of the income ceiling, they reduced their average work year by two-and-half weeks.[2]

Government controls also have caused misallocations of resources. While doctors are in short supply in remote regions, hospital beds are scarce mainly in urban centers. The government has reacted with more controls: Young doctors are penalized if they start their practice in an urban center. And the president of the Professional Corporation of Physicians has proposed drafting young medical school graduates to work in remote regions for a period of time.

Nationalization of the health industry also has led to increased centralization and politicization. Work stoppages by nurses and hospital workers have occurred half a dozen times over the last 20 years, and this does not include a few one-day strikes by doctors. Ambulance services and dispatching have been centralized under government control. As this article was being written, ambulance drivers and paramedics were working in jeans, they had covered their vehicles with protest stickers, and they were dangerously disrupting operations. The reason: They want the government to finish nationalizing what remains under private control in their industry.

When possible, doctors and nurses have voted with their feet. A personal anecdote will illustrate this. When my youngest son was born in California in 1978, the obstetrician was from Ontario and the nurse came from Saskatchewan. The only American-born in the delivery room was the baby.

When prices are zero, demand exceeds supply, and queues form. For many Canadians, hospital emergency rooms have become their primary doctor—as is the case with Medicaid patients in the United States. Patients lie in temporary beds in emergency rooms, sometimes for days. At Sainte-Justine Hospital, a major Montreal pediatric hospital, children often wait many hours before they can see a doctor. Surgery candidates face long waiting lists—it can take six months to have a cataract removed. Heart surgeons report patients dying while on their waiting lists. But then, it's free.

Or is it? The busy executive, housewife, or laborer has more productive things to do besides waiting in a hospital queue. For these people, waiting time carries a much higher cost than it does to the unemployed single person. So, if public health insurance reduces the costs of health services for some of the poor, it increases the costs for many other people. It discriminates against the productive.

The most visible consequence of socialized medicine in Canada is in the poor quality of services. Health care has become more and more impersonal. Patients often feel they are on an assembly line. Doctors and hospitals already have more patients than they can handle and no financial incentive to provide good service. Their customers are not the ones who write the checks anyway.

No wonder, then, that medicine in Quebec consumes only 9 percent of gross domestic product (7 percent if we consider only public expenditures) compared to some 11 percent in the United States. This does not indicate that health services are delivered efficiently at low cost. It reflects the fact that prices and remunerations in this industry are arbitrarily fixed, that services are rationed, and that individuals are forbidden to spend their medical-care dollars as they wish.

Is It Just?

Supporters of public health insurance reply that for all its inefficiencies, their system at least is more just. But even this isn't true.

Their conception of justice is based on the idea that certain goods like health (and education? and food? where do you stop?) should be made available to all through coercive redistribution by the state. If, on the contrary, we define justice in terms of liberty, then justice forbids coercing some (taxpayers, doctors, and nurses) into providing health services to others. Providing voluntarily for your neighbor in need may be morally good. Forcing your neighbor to help you is morally wrong.

Even if access to health services is a desirable objective, it is by no means clear that a socialized system is the answer. Without market rationing, queues form. There are ways to jump the queue, but they are not equally available to everyone.

In Quebec, you can be relatively sure not to wait six hours with your sick child in an emergency room if you know how to talk to the hospital director, or if one of your old classmates is a doctor, or if your children attend the same exclusive private school as your pediatrician's children. You may get good services if you deal with a medical clinic in the business district. And, of course, you will get excellent services if you fly to the Mayo Clinic in Minnesota or to some private hospital in Europe. The point is that these ways to jump the queue are pretty expensive for the typical lower-middle-class housewife, not to talk of the poor.

An Enquiry Commission on Health and Social Services submitted a thick report in December 1987, after having met for 30 months and spent many millions of dollars. It complains that "important gaps persist in matters of health and welfare among different groups."[3] Now, isn't this statement quite incredible after two decades of monopolistic socialized health care? Doesn't it show that equalizing conditions is an impossible task, at least when there is some individual liberty left?

One clear effect of a socialized health system is to increase the cost of getting above-average care (while the average is dropping). Some poor people, in fact, may obtain better care under socialized medicine. But many in the middle class will lose. It isn't clear where justice is to be found in such a redistribution.

There are two ways to answer the question: "What is the proper amount of medical care in different cases?" We may let private initiative and voluntary relations provide solutions. Or we may let politics decide. Health care has to be rationed either by the market or by political and bureaucratic processes. The latter are no more just than the former. We often forget that people who have difficulty making money in the market are not necessarily better at jumping queues in a socialized system.

There is no way to supply all medical services to everybody, for the cost would be astronomical. What do you do for a six-year-old Montreal girl with a rare form of leukemia who can be cured only in a Wisconsin hospital at a cost of $350,000—a real case? Paradoxically for a socialized health system, the family had to appeal to public charity, a more and more common occurrence. In the first two months, the family received more than $100,000 including a single anonymous donation of $40,000.

This is only one instance of health services that could have been covered by private health insurance but are being denied by hard-pressed public insurance. And the trend is getting worse. Imagine what will happen as the population ages.

There are private solutions to health costs. Insurance is one. Even in 1964, when insurance mechanisms were much less developed than today, 43 percent of the Quebec population carried private health insurance, and half of them had complete coverage. Today, most Americans not covered by Medicare or Medicaid carry some form of private health insurance. Private charity is another solution, so efficient that it has not been entirely replaced by the Canadian socialized system.

Can Trends Be Changed?

People in Quebec have grown so accustomed to socialized medicine that talks of privatization usually are limited to subcontracting hospital laundry or cafeteria services. The idea of subcontracting hospital management as a whole is deemed radical (although it is done on a limited scale elsewhere in Canada). There have been suggestions of allowing health maintenance organizations (HMOs) in Quebec, but the model would be that of Ontario, where HMOs are totally financed and controlled by the public health insurance system. The government of Quebec has repeatedly come out against for-profit HMOs.

Socialized medicine has had a telling effect on the public mind. In Quebec, 62 percent of the population now think that people should pay nothing to see a doctor; 82 percent want hospital care to remain free. People have come to believe that it is normal for the state to take care of their health.

Opponents of private health care do not necessarily quarrel with the efficiency of competition and private enterprise. They morally oppose the idea that some individuals may use money to purchase better health care. They prefer that everybody has less, provided it is equal. *The Gazette,* one of Montreal's English newspapers, ran an editorial arguing that gearing the quality of health care to the ability to pay "is morally and socially unacceptable."[4]

The idea that health care should be equally distributed is part of a wider egalitarian culture. Health is seen as one of the goods of life that need to be socialized. The Quebec Enquiry Commission on Health and Social Services was quite clear on this:

> The Commission believes that the reduction of these inequalities and more generally the achievement of fairness in the fields of health and welfare must be one of the first goals of the system and direct all its interventions. It is clear that the health

and social services system is not the only one concerned. This concern applies as strongly to labor, the environment, education and income security.[5]

A Few Lessons

Several lessons can be drawn from the Canadian experience with socialized medicine.

First of all, socialized medicine, although of poor quality, is very expensive. Public health expenditures consume close to 7 percent of the Canadian gross domestic product, and account for much of the difference between the levels of public expenditure in Canada (47 percent of gross domestic product) and in the U.S. (37 percent of gross domestic product). So if you do not want a large public sector, do not nationalize health.

A second lesson is the danger of political compromise. One social policy tends to lead to another. Take, for example, the introduction of publicly funded hospital insurance in Canada. It encouraged doctors to send their patients to hospitals because it was cheaper to be treated there. The political solution was to nationalize the rest of the industry. Distortions from one government intervention often lead to more intervention.

A third lesson deals with the impact of egalitarianism. Socialized medicine is both a consequence and a great contributor to the idea that economic conditions should be equalized by coercion. If proponents of public health insurance are not challenged on this ground, they will win this war and many others. Showing that human inequality is both unavoidable and, within the context of equal formal rights, desirable, is a long-run project. But then, as Saint-Exupéry wrote, "Il est vain, si l'on plante un chêne, d'espérer s'abriter bientôt sous son feuillage."[6]

---

1. Report of the Enquiry Commission on Health and Social Services, Government of Quebec, 1988, pp. 148, 339.

2. Gérard Bélanger, "Les dépenses de santé par rapport à l'économie du Québec," *Le Médecin du Québec,* December 1981, p. 37.

3. Report of the Enquiry Commission on Health and Social Services, p. 446 (our translation).

4. "No Second Class Patients," editorial of *The Gazette,* May 21, 1988.

5. Report of the Enquiry Commission on Health and Social Services, p. 446 (our translation).

6. "It is a vain hope, when planting an oak tree, to hope to soon take shelter under it."

National Health Care: Medicine in Germany 1918–1945

by Marc S. Micozzi, M.D.

Today we are concerned about issues such as doctor-assisted suicide, abortion, the use of fetal tissue, genetic screening, birth control and sterilization, health care rationing and the ethics of medical research on animals and humans. These subjects are major challenges in both ethics and economics at the end of the twentieth century. But at the beginning of the twentieth century the desire to create a more scientific medical practice and research had already raised the issues of euthanasia, eugenics, and medical experimentation on human subjects. In addition, the increasing involvement of the German government in medical care and funding medical research established the government-medical complex that the National Socialists later used to execute their extermination policies.

The German social insurance and health care system began in the 1880s under Bismarck. Ironically, it was part of Bismarck's "anti-socialist" legislation, adopted under the theory that a little socialism would prevent the rise of a more virulent socialism.

By the time of Weimar, German doctors had become accustomed to cooperating with the government in the provision of medical care. The reforms of the Weimar Republic following the medical crises of World War I included government policies to provide health care services to all citizens. Socially minded physicians placed great hope in a new health care system, calling for a single state agency to overcome fragmentation and the lack of influence of individual practitioners and local services. The focus of medicine shifted from private practice to public health and from treating disease to preventable health care. During the German "economic consolidation" of 1924–1928, public

Marc S. Micozzi, M.D., Ph.D., a physician and anthropologist, directs the National Museum of Health and Medicine in Washington, D.C., which recently brought from Berlin the exhibition, "The Value of the Human Being: Medicine in Germany 1918–1945." This article was written for the November 1993 issue of *The Freeman*.

health improved under new laws against tuberculosis, venereal disease, and alcoholism, with new advisory centers for chemical dependency and counselling bureaus for marriage and sexual problems.

Medical concerns which had largely been in the private domain in the nineteenth century increasingly became a concern of the state. The physician began to be transformed into a functionary of state-initiated laws and policies. Doctors slowly began to see themselves as more responsible for the public health of the nation than for the individual health of the patient. It is one thing to see oneself as responsible for the "nation's health" and quite another to be responsible for the individual patient's health. It is one thing to be employed by an individual, another to be employed by the government.

Under the Weimar Republic these reforms resulted in clearly improved public health. However, the creativity, energy, and fundamental reforms found in social medicine during the Weimar Republic seem in retrospect a short and deceptive illusion. Medical reformers had wanted to counter the misery inherited from the first World War and the Second Empire on the basis of comprehensive disease prevention programs. In the few years available to the social reformers, they had remarkable success. But in connection with these reforms the doctor's role changed from that of advocate, adviser, and partner of the patient to a partner of the state.

Where traditional individual ethics and Christian charity had once stood, the reformers posited a collective ethic for the benefit of the general population. Private charity and welfare were nationalized. The mentally ill, for example, having been literally released from their chains in the nineteenth century and placed in local communities and boarding houses in regular contact with others (the so-called "moral therapy"), were returned to state institutions to become the ultimate victims of state "solutions."

With the world economic crisis of 1929, welfare state expenditures had to be reduced for housing, nutrition, support payments, recreation and rehabilitation, and maternal and child health. What remained of the humanistic goals of reform were state mechanisms for inspection and regulation of public health and medical practice. Economic efficiency became the major concern, and health care became primarily a question of cost-benefit analysis. Under the socialist policies of the period, this analysis was necessarily applied to the selection of strong persons, deemed worthy of support, and the elimination of weak and "unproductive" people. The scientific underpinning of cost-benefit analyses to political medical care was provided by the new fields of genetics and eugenics.

Genetics and Eugenics

At the same time as these economic and political developments, the application of nineteenth-century scientific discoveries began to make their way into twentieth-century public health and medical practice. Charles Darwin's studies on natural selection were of course based upon animal populations living in nature and not human populations living in complex societies. But the biological basis of natural selection gave rise to a concept of "survival of the fittest" in human civilizations. This term was coined by the British social anthropologist Herbert Spencer, and the concept led to "Social Darwinism."

Darwin's theories (developed in parallel with Alfred Russel Wallace—another British natural scientist) had been published prior to full elucidation of the principles of genetics. With subsequent understanding and acceptance of the science of genetics, the underlying basis of natural selection could more completely be described. While scientists still did not understand what made up the gene (awaiting Watson and Crick's discovery of DNA in the 1950s) they began to search for outward expression of inner genetic tendencies. In the absence of being able to pinpoint individual genes, they sought outward expression of genetic "types." These "typologies" were largely based upon external measurements of the body.

Much of this work was carried out by German anthropologists and physicians (often one and the same at that time) in newly acquired colonies in German East and Southwest Africa, prior to the loss of these colonies to Allied protectorates in World War I. Such work resumed following the war, however, and by 1927 the opening of the Kaiser Wilhelm Institute of Anthropology, Human Genetics, and Eugenics was celebrated in Berlin as the advent of the "German Oxford." The annual report of the Institute in 1932 stated: "The term eugenics means to establish a connection between the results of the studies in human genetics and practical measures in population policy."

Under the new "scientific understanding" of human biology provided by genetics and its implementation under eugenics, poverty, for example, would become merely an expression of degeneracy *(Entartung)* and genetic inferiority. "Inferior" and "superior" became natural terms used by persons of nearly all political persuasions, as readily as the terms "handicapped," "impaired," "socially dependent" or "disadvantaged" are used today.

Life Unworthy of Living

Following World War I there had been concern among some in Germany that the war had decimated the ranks of the qualified and strong while weak, unqualified, and inferior people had been spared. Many felt that scant resources should not be wasted on the sick and suffering. The philosophy of the unimportance of the individual in favor of the people *(Das Volk)* led to the belief that individuals who had become "worthless, defective parts" had to be "sacrificed or discarded."

Alfred Hoche, a neuropathologist (as Freud had been) and Karl Binding, a lawyer, published a pamphlet in 1922, *The Sanctioning of the Destruction of Life Unworthy of Living*. Binding relativized the legal and moral prohibition, "Thou shalt not kill," and Hoche alternated between economic and medical arguments. Neurologists in Saxony formally discussed the topic, "Are Doctors Allowed to Kill?" A physician in Dresden pointed out "the contradiction that many persons (reformers) demand an end to the death penalty for crimes, but the same people are for putting imbeciles [*sic*] to death." By the time the National Socialist Party came to power in Germany, the mentally ill and the mentally retarded had begun to be sterilized and to be subjected to euthanasia in large numbers in German government institutions.

National Socialism and the Nation's Health

No profession in Germany became so numerically attached to National Socialism in both its leadership and membership as was the medical profession. Because of their philosophical orientation toward finding a more scientific basis for medical research and practice, government funding for research, and the practical benefits of acquiring university positions and medical practices from the the many banned and exiled German Jewish doctors, many physicians supported Nazi policies. One of the first Nazi laws, passed July 14, 1933, was the "Law for the Prevention of Progeny of Hereditary Disease," intended to "consolidate" social and health policies in the German population and prohibit the right of reproduction for persons defined as "genetically inferior." After 1933, the connection between the theory and practice of politicized medicine advocated by many in Weimar Germany became actual in Nazi Germany.

A "Genetic Health Court" consisting of judges and doctors made decisions about forcible sterilization. As "advocates of the state," doctors prosecuted those persons charged with being "genetically ill" in sessions lasting generally no more than ten minutes and from which the public was barred. In 1935, an adjunct law allowed forcible abortion in such cases up to the sixth month of pregnancy. A total of 300,000 to 400,000 were sterilized and approximately 5,000 (nearly all women) died as a result of these operations. After 1945, it was argued to the Restitution Claims Commission of the German Bundestag that the "Law for the Prevention of Progeny of Hereditary Disease" not be considered in the same category as subsequent National Socialist race laws and other Nazi abuses. The sterilization law had been drafted earlier under the Weimar Republic as part of progressive health reform, and as late as 1961 was defended by an expert at the Max Planck Institute on the basis that "every cultured nation needs eugenics, and in the atomic age, more so than ever before."

German Youth and Euthanasia

Following the sterilization laws, the National Socialists next implemented a strategy of euthanasia to solve the remaining problems of those whose conception and birth had preceded these laws. The pediatrician Ernst Wentzler, while developing plans to improve care in the German Children's Hospitals in Berlin, personally decided (as consultant to Hitler's Chancellery) on the deaths of thousands of handicapped children. Hans Nachtsheim placed delivery orders for handicapped children for his pressure chamber experiments on epilepsy. Joseph Mengele delivered genetic and anthropological "material" from Auschwitz to the Kaiser Wilhelm Institute and conducted his infamous twin experiments on the child victims of the Holocaust.

Julius Hallervorden at the Kaiser Wilhelm Institute for Brain Research at Berlin-Buch carried out several research projects based on euthanasia programs. Hallervorden and others systematically collected the brains of their patients who had been killed, taught the murdering doctors how to dissect, and cooperated closely with institutions where murdered children had previously been given thorough examinations and tests. During interrogation by an American officer in 1945, he stated, "I heard that they were going to do that . . . and told them . . . if you are going to kill all these people, at least take the brains. . . . There was wonderful material among these brains—beautiful mental defectives, malformations and early infantile disease. I accepted these brains, of course. Where they came from and how they came to me, was really none of my business." The collection was until recently kept by the Max Planck Institute (formerly the Kaiser Wilhelm Institute) in Frankfurt and used for brain research.

Human Experimentation

In a system in which so many were routinely condemned to die, the temptation proved strong to use human subjects in medical experimentation prior to their tragic and terrible deaths.

The Luftwaffe had developed aircraft which could climb to altitudes of nearly 60,000 feet, altitudes unattainable by Allied fighter aircraft. However, tolerance of these altitudes on the part of pilots had not yet been tested. Trials on volunteers at altitudes above 36,000 feet had to be discontinued due to severe pain. For this reason, lethal altitude experiments in pressure chambers were conducted on 200 victims held prisoner in Dachau concentration camp in a program called: "Trials for Saving Persons at High Altitude."

Many German ships were also being sunk in the North Atlantic and North Sea, and the same group of medical investigators conducted painful ice bath experiments on 300 Dachau prisoners in a research program entitled "Avoidance and Treatment of Hypothermia in Water." Other medical experiments were carried out with chemical and biological warfare agents and infectious diseases.

Follow World War II much of this data was kept classified by Allied military authorities on the basis of national security. Debate continues to this day on the validity of these experiments and the ethical implications of any use of such data.

The Banality of Evil

We now know the end of this historical horror story of massive crimes against humanity and the leader of the thousand-year Reich burning in a bunker in Berlin. But it is not so easy to recognize the steps on the path down the slippery slope when we don't yet know the end of the story—as today we do not know which social health reforms in combination with which new medical technologies have the potential to plunge modern society over a brink in which disaster might result. Is legalized abortion a new form of medicide? Is doctor-assisted suicide a step toward positive euthanasia? Is modern genetic testing and the Human Genome Project the first step to a new eugenics? Is health care rationing, which is always a result of government involvement in medical care, a step toward the new definition of "life unworthy of living"? Is our present "quality of life index" a new way of saying it?

Nazi medicine was implemented by a political-medical complex—on the basis of political health care—a scientific and social philosophy imposed by a totalitarian regime. It should never happen again, but could it ever happen again?

In the United States the medical profession operates in a mixed (not a national socialist) economy which does not yet have the institutionalized mechanisms of control and regulation of Weimar Germany—and in a democratic political system which thankfully does not have the political ideology of the Third Reich. But the "banality of evil" described by Hannah Arendt in the Third Reich may stem largely from a government bureaucracy in which 90 percent of the people think 90 percent of the time about process—not purpose. Does the modern bureaucratization of medicine hold any real risk for a possible return—with new health reforms and new medical technologies—to some of the horrors of National Socialist medicine? Removal of personal responsibility ("I was only following orders"), personal authority, and personal choice in a bureaucratized system may leave less and less room for individual ethics in the conduct of medical science and practice.

Politicized medicine is not a sufficient cause of the mass extermination of human beings, but it seems to be a necessary cause. The Nazi Holocaust did not happen for some inexplicable German reason; it is not an event that we can afford to ignore because we are not Germans or not Nazis. The history of Germany from 1914 to 1945 is a telescoping of modernity—from monarchy, war, and collapse to democracy and the welfare state, and finally to dictatorship, war, and death.

Medical ethics is the responsibility of all members of a society, not just doctors and scientists. Medicine and science alone do not have the answers to such questions as: When does life begin? When should it end? Are humans just the sum of their genetic parts or genetic programs? While bioethicists debate, individual medical choices are made a million times a day among doctors, patients, their families, and increasingly the government. The product of all these choices ultimately constitutes the ethical, legal, and social framework in which the practice of medicine and of medical research are conducted. In the end it is the preservation of freedom that will guide us to the best application of new health reforms and technologies in the future.

Health Planning in Fort Wayne—
The Six Million Dollar Fizzle

by Joe Hochderffer

Federal health planning has cost our community more than six million dollars in inflated construction costs, a two-year denial of needed hospital facilities, and a confused, divided citizenry.

This year the Northern Indiana Health Systems Agency, a creature of Public Law 93–641, the health planning law, expects to become one of the nation's first HSAs to receive "full designation" as a health planning agency by HEW.

The Fort Wayne story began shortly after federal health planning became the law of the land. This was the result of a 1971 law, P.L. 92–603, which created Health Planning Councils. P.L. 92–603 was passed to correct the blunders of a previous Congress which, in 1965, created Medicare and Medicaid.

In the summer of 1973 Fort Wayne was a placid community of 170,000 people earning higher than average incomes and served by six shopping centers, five McDonald's, two Holiday Inns, and three general community hospitals. Not one in a thousand residents was aware that his tax dollars supported the newly formed Health Planning Council (HPC), staffed by a handful of planners and secretaries whose paychecks came circuitously from HEW.

The health planners were making speeches about the plan they were going to create for our nine-county Health Planning Area when, suddenly, two separate groups of physicians presented them with proposals to build additional hospitals in Fort Wayne. The need for additional facilities was well known to a community accustomed to overflowing hospitals.

Federal procedure called for the planners to consider whether or

Mr. Hochderffer, a hospital administrator in Indiana, wrote this article for the August 1977 issue of *Private Practice*. It was reprinted by permission in the December 1977 issue of *The Freeman*.

not a proposal fit the overall community health plan. And there was no such plan. So the planners determined within a few weeks that Fort Wayne needed 156 medical-surgical beds.

A Health Planning Council, which by law must be composed of more health care "consumers" than "providers," started a series of deliberations. After weeks of testimony and hearings, the consumer-dominated body approved one proposal and forwarded it to the State Board of Health for final action. The other they sent to the State Board of Health without recommendation. Thus a local controversy was transferred to the State Board of Health for resolution.

The state board dug out its guidelines and discovered that any proposal it approved must conform to a state plan, which was a creature of the Hill-Burton Act. Under the state plan, Fort Wayne was allotted three hospitals—and they already existed.

"What about those three hospitals?" the state board asked. "Did they plan to do anything about the hospital bed shortage in Fort Wayne?"

As a matter of fact, they did.

Head Start

Each hospital had expansion plans on the drawing boards when the health planning legislation was passed. Being more familiar with the law than others (because they had to be), the hospitals had been waiting for the HPC to develop its master plan before submitting expansion proposals.

Now the State Board of Health asked the hospitals if they could add 156 beds more economically than could the backers of new hospitals.

Yes, they could.

The reason was simple: New hospitals had to build laboratories, X-ray departments, kitchens, pharmacies, and laundries to serve their beds; existing hospitals already had such ancillary services and needed only to utilize them more fully or enlarge them.

During the next several months as the local HPC again went through a long series of meetings to consider plans of the existing hospitals, promoters of new hospitals debated board members and administrators of existing hospitals. And the public got a picture of three giant hospitals conspiring to gain a monopoly and to strangle any attempt to build a fourth hospital in Fort Wayne.

The public still had the idea that we were under the free enterprise system. They believed that if a group of people wanted to build a hospital, and had the wherewithal to do it, they should be able to.

The public was not aware that when it turned the hospital care of its senior citizens over to Medicare free enterprise went out the window. If you do not get HPC approval of your capital outlays, the law states, you cannot count those expenditures as legitimate costs when the government reimburses you for Medicare/Medicaid patients.

So existing hospitals and backers of new ones were forced to seek HPC approval for new facilities. Since there was a magic quota fixed by master planners on the number of beds needed, existing hospitals could win only at the expense of new hospitals, and new hospitals could win only if old hospitals were denied expansion plans. What was in reality a battle of "hospitals versus federal quotas" appeared to be "hospitals versus hospitals."

Action Delayed

When the smoke cleared six months later, existing hospitals were allowed to expand. They could add new beds more economically than a new hospital could build them.

But that was not the stated reason for the decision. The stated reason was that the state plan called for only three hospitals in Fort Wayne and therefore a fourth one could not be built. This seemed ridiculous to a public that had had no previous knowledge of health planning laws and regulations.

There followed two years of lawsuits by new hospital backers, during which time existing hospitals were enjoined from carrying out expansion plans. And inflation hurried on, unrestrained.

The appeals process was not exhausted until late 1976, when the fourth hospital backers had clearly lost. Nobody in Fort Wayne felt good about the whole matter. I work for one of the existing hospitals, the alleged winners, and there's a dirty taste in my mouth.

True, our present three hospitals can build and operate new beds more economically than could a new hospital. But the federal planning process created a divided medical staff at our hospital, caused bitter animosities within the community, wasted thousands of hours and millions of dollars, and after four years has not yet produced a single new hospital bed in Fort Wayne.

That was all under the old planning law, 92–603. Now we have a new law, P.L. 93–641, that is much more restrictive.

It mandates "consumer" domination of HSA boards. On the surface this is not much different from P.L. 92–603. That law required "consumers" to compose at least 51 percent of planning boards; "providers" of health care (doctors, dentists, nurses, hospital administrators) composed the remaining 49 percent. A "provider" was defined as anyone who derived a major portion of his income from providing health services. The new law is different. It broadens the definition of "provider" to include anyone who has even remote connections with a medical institution. Hospital board members, for example, who usually serve without pay and who derive their income from other sources, are classified as "providers." People who sell health insurance are "providers." Thus the effect of the new law is to insure domination on planning agency boards of persons wholly ignorant of medical care. In practice, these people become dependent upon the professional planners employed by HEW to guide them in the decision-making process.

A New Base of Power

The new law further removes the power base from the local community. P.L. 92–603 had shifted the planning base from the community to a multi-county district. P.L. 93–641 eliminates these small districts and creates large ones. Our HSA covers one-third of Indiana, from the Chicago suburbs to the farmlands of northeastern Indiana.

P.L. 93–641 mandates planning. No hospital (or any other business) ever survived without planning, so what's new? Now the planning must meet the approval of HEW bureaucrats.

The new law eventually substitutes federal power for state power. Under previous laws, final decision-making was done by state boards of health. Under P.L. 93–641, as soon as the HSA receives "full designation," it becomes the final authority.

Ours was one of the three Fort Wayne hospitals asked to submit plans and cost estimates for adding beds back when the Health Planning Council was considering applications for new hospitals in the city. On our drawing boards at that time (1973) was a large project to expand certain service departments such as X-ray, laboratory, and dietary which our hospital had outgrown. We were also considering additional beds, but those plans were not as well-developed nor was the need so pressing as that of the ancillary department expansion.

An Efficient Business

In its 20-year history our hospital had grown from 250 beds to a 600-bed regional referral center. We were one of the most successful and financially sound hospitals in the nation. We had consistently operated at high occupancy (over 90 percent), had engaged in six expansion projects and paid for them without incurring major debt, and were charging our patients $10 a day below the state average and $30 a day under national averages. In American Hospital Association records we could find no hospital in our class operating so inexpensively as we were.

In 1970 we had added 56 beds and paid for them out of operations. In 1973 we needed to expand ancillary departments to handle the increased capacity, as well as the burgeoning growth of outpatient business.

When the planners asked us how much it would cost to add new beds, we had to speed up the planning process for beds and delay the ancillary expansion plans. We asked if we should submit both proposals at once, because our most pressing need was for ancillary, not bed, expansion.

No, said the planners, that would cloud the issue. Just tell us how much the beds would cost.

Okay, we said, but we can't add beds without expanding service departments. The new beds will mean that we must enlarge our ancillary areas slightly more than our existing plans call for. How will we show that in our proposal for new beds?

Just take a percentage of your ancillary expansion needs and tack that onto your bed proposal, said the planners.

So we did. It was backwards planning as far as we were concerned, but we did it the way the planners told us.

Our bed proposal was approved, including the percentages of upcoming ancillary expansion, plans which had not yet been submitted. Then followed the two years of lawsuits and injunctions, during which time we had undersized service departments to accommodate growing numbers of patients. We could not proceed with ancillary expansion, because the size of that expansion depended on whether or nor we received final approval for the new beds.

New Planners for Old

During the waiting period, P.L. 93–641 replaced P.L. 92–603 as the federal health planning law. Old health planning boards were replaced with large new ones. New bureaucrats moved into the wealth of new federal jobs created. And when the court decision finally freed us to add the beds, we faced a new agency with a new set of rules in trying to get approval for ancillary expansion.

We brought our ancillary expansion proposal before them.

Our hospital, with its one part-time planner (me), faced a new agency with a staff of 25 planners.

"How many meals do you produce per square foot?" they asked. "Why is the volume of X-rays performed so much higher on the day shift than on the night shift? Can you fully document the need for 2,750 more square feet of surgery? Why not 1,375 square feet?"

Thus began a six-month ordeal to try to get facilities to serve patients who had been denied them too long.

What evolved was an 80-page application plus a 40-page financial feasibility study conducted by independent auditors. The fourth draft of this document was accepted as adequate.

Following federal guidelines to the letter, we met with the HSA staff a given number of days before the board hearing was to be held. They informed us that the staff would recommend our project be rejected.

Why? we asked.

Because it does not meet federal mandates to contain costs, they replied.

But, we protested, our hospital has the best cost record in the country. It would seem that you would want to encourage operations such as ours.

True, they said, you have a good cost record. But we have no assurance that it will continue.

During the next hour our board members and administration made almost no impression on the HSA staff. So we decided to take our case to their board anyway.

Our presentation before the board convinced them that our project was deserving and financially feasible. We were able to demonstrate that, even with proposed expansion, our square footages were below the ranges the planners had used. Even with construction and financing costs added, our rates would still be far under state and national averages.

The board went against its own staff and approved us.

But, we were to discover, the fight had just begun.

Proposal Rejected

The group that endorsed our project was known as a "sub-area council." The next step was to get approval before the executive committee of the Northern Indiana Health Systems Agency. This was a small committee, most of whose members lived more than a hundred miles from our community and whose allegiance to the professional planners was unmistakable.

The hearing was held 70 miles from home. The procedure allowed no presentation on our part. We were permitted to answer questions, but nothing else. It took less than 10 minutes for them to dispose of us. Our proposal was rejected.

We had one more chance.

At this point the HSA had only "recommending" authority. The final decision still rested with the State Board of Health. Our alternatives were either to take our application to the State Board of Health—with one "approval" and one "disapproval" on our record—or withdraw it, as the planners hinted we should do, and revise it.

Our inclination was to go to the State Board. These were reasonable people who were familiar with our hospital. Surely we could get a fair shake.

But the federal procedure stated that if an applicant is turned down by the state agency, it cannot submit the proposal again for three years. Our patients had already waited three years, should we gamble?

Through unofficial channels we tried to get a feel as to how the State Board of Health viewed our proposal. What we learned was frightening.

Subsidy Means Control

The State Board was intimidated. Much of the State Health Department's funding comes from federal sources. And the word was that if the state didn't go along with the federal recommendations, there would be serious questions raised about federal funding in other areas of operations.

We learned (unofficially) that our project didn't stand a chance.

So we withdrew it, as the planners had suggested. Our next step was to meet with them and learn the surrender terms.

In a two-hour conference with the top HSA officials, we asked what it was in our application that should be reduced or eliminated. Should we, for example, scale down the dietary department or surgery, or what?

The director merely looked over our heads at the light fixtures. We were patiently reminded of federal concern over medical costs and gently scolded for not being more cooperative with the planning staff. After a series of hints and innuendoes, we finally got the picture.

"Cut at least 10 percent from the costs. We don't care where or how you do it. Just cut the dollars."

On the surface this sounds reasonable. Federal planners insisting that those inefficient, gouge-the-public hospitals reduce their expenditures. Who could quarrel with that?

But our hospital was not inefficient. Its cost record was documented and known. It had demonstrated at the public hearing that if it were to become "average" (and thus fit all the planners' guidelines) it would spend an extra $8 million in operating costs in two years, nearly enough to finance the proposed building project.

We had learned our lesson, however. The federal planners now called the tune. No longer did our hospital board determine the institution's destiny. What counted was how close the hospital could come to the "averages" used in planners' reference guides.

The purpose of the average is, presumably, to bring below-average hospitals up to par. The effect is also to bring above-average hospitals, such as ours, down to par.

In order to get the needed facilities, we played the game.

The cuts made in our project were designed to please the planners, not to make good economic or operational sense. The planners, in effect, wrote our new application for us. We ground out more reams of data—laboratory procedures per square foot, man hours per meal, *ad infinitum*. It was the same material we've done before, only turned upside down to please the bureaucrats.

The HSA staff approved us this time. The sub-area council okayed us (for a second time) and the executive committee gave us unanimous approval. Now we can build; we've paid the ransom.

In the spring of 1977 we broke ground on a project that, without the federal planning laws, would have been started in 1974. Construction costs had been escalating at one percent per month all that time. We'll have to build these inflated costs into our charge structure. (And guess whom the public will blame?)

Today in Fort Wayne $27 million in construction is underway by three hospitals. If hospital boards (much more local in composition and with a greater ratio of consumers than the HSA boards) had determined the construction starts, rather than governmental agencies, more than $6 million could have been saved.

Many Fort Wayne citizens still believe that the three existing hospitals kept a fourth hospital from opening in their community. That the public itself allowed federal intervention, through Medicare and health planning laws, to stifle free enterprise, they do not believe.

In the rest of the nation HSAs are not yet in full operation. But the mandate is clear. The federal planners will absolutely control hospital development. They will not save money, they will waste it.

They will achieve only one thing: control. And that's what they're after.

III. THE INAPTITUDES OF POLITICS

The Coming Push for National Health Care

by Terree P. Wasley

Conservatives and free-marketeers across the country have cause to celebrate these days. For the first time in decades, Congress has eliminated a welfare-state program. Repealing the catastrophic care plan for the elderly has raised hopes that future spending sprees on health care will face insurmountable opposition in Congress. Health-care experts, journalists, and broadcast commentators have advised that other forays by the government into health issues, such as man-dated benefits, long-term or nursing home care, national health insur-ance, and nationalized health care are virtually dead in the water. *The Wall Street Journal* even remarked that this recent defeat has killed for now any further attempts to socialize American medicine.

Despite this remarkable success in rolling back one program, now is *not* the time for those who believe in free markets to relax. If current wisdom is correct, then the Bush Administration has a unique window of opportunity through which to propose major reforms to this coun-try's ailing health-care system, bringing it back into balance with our free-market convictions. The time may be right to urge significant changes that would curtail spiraling health-care costs, making health care more affordable and offering citizens the chance to choose the way to provide for their own future health-care needs.

The Administration must act now, for to wait may allow an op-portunity to pass that might never come again. Those who believe government can best provide for our lives are already working behind the scenes for passage of a comprehensive national health-care plan for *all* Americans—and their target date is 1990.

Calls for some kind of national health-care program have increased during the past year and are coming from a variety of sources. The

Ms. Wasley, an economist and consultant based in Phoenix, Arizona, is the author of *What Has Government Done to Our Health Care?* (Cato Institute, 1992). This article origi-nally appeared in *The Freeman,* January 1990.

rapid escalation in health-care costs, particularly in the 1980s, and attention to the fact that approximately 30 million Americans lack health care insurance, have raised demands for some kind of universal solution.

Not too surprisingly, the A.F.L.-C.I.O. used its national convention in November to kick off a major campaign for national health insurance legislation in the next Congress. However, what has amazed some are voices from the business community speaking out for more federal government involvement in health care. Ever-rising health-care costs, due to government interference and a perverse system of incentives and controls,[1] have so frustrated American business leaders that some have now resigned themselves to failure and are asking the government to bail them out.

Art Puccini, vice president at General Electric, in a speech early last year said, "Rising employee medical costs may lead some of us who today are free-market advocates to re-examine our thinking and positions with respect to government-sponsored national health insurance." Ford Motor Company has been using its seat on President Bush's Competitiveness Council to push for government health care, and General Motors vice president Beach Hall has been seen at several recent Capitol Hill meetings on the issue.

Walter B. Maher, director of employee benefits for Chrysler Corporation, has urged that a national budget be set for health care each year—much like in Canada, Britain, and other countries with national health-care plans. The Washington Business Group on Health, which represents about 180 Fortune 500 companies on health issues, is one of several groups drafting a national health-care plan with the goal of controlling health-related spending.

Astonishingly, it's not just big business, frustrated with mounting health-care costs, that is turning a favorable eye toward a national health plan. A recent Dun & Bradstreet survey of *small* business found that 38 percent favored some form of national health insurance. The Independent Business Federation says 15 percent of its members polled in 1989 would agree to a mandatory national health insurance program.

In addition to business, another unlikely group has joined the clamor for national health care: physicians. Last year, Physicians for a National Health Program, a two-year-old group of 1,200 doctors from across the U.S., proposed a single public insurance plan that would pay for all approved medical services. According to Dr. Arnold Relman, editor-in-chief of the *New England Journal of Medicine,* "Nothing short of a comprehensive plan is likely to achieve the goals of universal access, cost containment and preservation of quality that everyone seems to want."

Many experts believe that it is currently impossible to undertake a national health-care program of any kind, because of federal budget deficits. Despite this, polls are showing that Americans see the deficit as less and less of a threat and that they are concerned about those who don't have access to health care because of its current high costs. Because of that concern, and if skyrocketing health costs are not slowed, some health-care experts, such as Harvard University professor Robert J. Blendon, predict that national health care will become a major issue during the next few years.

Socialized medicine, the phrase normally used for a national care program, conjures up vivid images in most Americans' minds. One sees Soviet citizens dying because of a lack of adequate medical care, British citizens waiting for months to undergo a simple procedure or surgery, rich Europeans paying under the table to get their names pushed to the top of a waiting list, and Canadians hopping the border into the U.S. to have procedures done, rather than wait months or maybe years in their homeland.

No one, including most members of Congress, expects the American people to accept a socialized system like that of the Soviets, with its centralized control of every aspect of health care. Recent attention given to the severe problems besieging the British national health care system has prompted Prime Minister Thatcher to institute some market-based reforms and has turned proponents away from that example. However, many bills recently introduced in Congress would provide for a system of national health insurance modeled after the perceived success of the Canadian health-care system.

One of the bills receiving the most attention is Senator Kennedy's "Minimum Health Benefits for All Workers Act." This bill would require all employers to provide health care insurance for workers and their dependents. Besides being a major intrusion by the government into individual and business decisions, the bill would increase health insurance costs by $100 billion, result in a loss of one million jobs, and spawn a further escalation in medical price inflation. One cannot overlook that mandated benefits are really transfer payments in disguise, with all the pernicious economic consequences of such transfers. A study by the National Center for Policy Analysis estimates that as many as 25 percent of the uninsured lack health coverage because current state-mandated benefit laws make it too expensive.

Governor Michael Dukakis has been touting his new Massachusetts universal health insurance program as a model for the nation, and politicians in some states have believed him. Under the Massachusetts program, all companies with more than five employees that don't provide insurance are required to contribute as much as $1,680 a year for each employee to a pool providing health insurance to people without coverage. Interestingly, a year after the plan has gone into effect, it is facing severe budget shortfalls, and hospitals and businesses are concerned they will be left footing the bill for skyrocketing costs.

Many politicians have praised the Canadian system of health care as successful in providing satisfactory health care at lower costs than the United States. But the problems inherent in any health system based on social insurance or direct government funding are already showing up in the Canadian program. These endemic flaws should give pause to U.S. lawmakers eager to adopt a plan similar to the Canadian one.

The underlying problem with any social insurance system is that patients make little or no contribution to the cost of their care. What follows is the exorbitant increase in the demand for health care services, and the resulting price controls, rationing, income controls on physicians, shortages of equipment, deterioration of medical facilities, and long waiting lists. Canada has exhibited all of these symptoms, and many Canadians routinely cross the border into the U.S. for treatment. Price controls, rationing, and waiting lists do put a lid on health care spending, and that is exactly why many politicians can boast that Canada spends less on health care than the United States. But is that the quality of health care Americans want?

As mentioned above, a unique window of opportunity may exist in Washington following the collapse of the catastrophic health care legislation. Now is the time to reverse the trend toward nationalizing our health care system and replace it with a free market. The creation of Medicare and Medicaid in the 1960s, their continued expansion, and the addition of a crazy quilt of health care programs by both the federal and state governments have virtually destroyed Americans' access to reasonable and efficient health care.

Government intervention has our health-care system caught in a vicious cycle of government-encouraged demand that drives up costs, bankrupts federal and state budgets, and leads to still more infusions of money and program expansions that encourage additional consumption. Only the elimination of government interference and a return to a free market in health care will end the move toward nationalization. Only a free market will break the spiral of ever-increasing medical costs. As Ludwig von Mises wrote, "The pricing process of the unhampered market directs production into those channels in which it best serves the wishes of the consumers as manifested on the market."[2] Only a free market in health care will allow individuals maximum choice in meeting their health-care needs.

---

1. For a detailed history of our health care system, see *Critical Issues: A National Health System for America,* edited by Stuart M. Butler and Edmund F. Haislmaier (Washington, D.C.: The Heritage Foundation, 1989), chapter 1.

2. Ludwig von Mises, *Human Action: A Treatise on Economics* (Chicago: Contemporary Books, 1966), p. 394.

Free Medicine Can Make You Sick

by Charles G. Jones, M.D.

Among the socialistic wedges being driven into the heart of our openly competitive society is government-controlled medicine. Its advocates describe it in glowing colors. "It is the moral obligation of a civilized nation," they maintain, "to care for the indigent, aged, infirm, physically handicapped, and mentally ill." They talk as if only the state could discharge this obligation. In my belief, government medical care unwittingly prolongs the suffering of those already ill, and even causes illness to develop.

A widespread public complacency reflects lack of serious thought as to the possible consequences of socialized medicine in the United States. Many are lulled by a false sense of security because they hear so much about the benefits and so little, if anything, about the costs—the price to be paid. Experiences from other countries which have tried socialize medicine are depressing and alarming and ought to guide us away from similar mistakes.

One of the most glaring facts is that government medical care invariably costs more than had been expected. During the first four years of socialized medicine in Great Britain, the demands for free service and for costly though often unnecessary medically related items resulted in trebling the yearly budget. The taxpayer—who still has to foot the bill—had his annual tax burden increased by 12 percent. This on top of already heavy taxes makes the system almost prohibitive.

The deleterious effects of the system are to be noted everywhere. There are so many free dental patients that dentists no longer have time for their customary work with school children. Obviously, this condition need persist for very few years to affect seriously the dental health of the kingdom. Waiting lists for admission to hospitals became staggering. The increased volume of patients invites second-rate care

Dr. Jones is a surgeon in Grove City, Pennsylvania. This article appeared in the February 1958 *Freeman*.

for many instead of first-rate care for the truly ill. The burdensome cost of caring for those who are ill, plus those who pretend, leaves no funds for research or preventive medicine. Along with the details of administration, there is the problem of selecting from the long lists the patient who needs immediate or emergency care. The system not only involves huge cost, but it also constitutes a menace rather than a means to health. In other words, "You cannot buy good health."

The Voluntary Way

Even though the American system is still voluntary, in that hospital and health insurance can be selected at will, some of these evils are beginning to make themselves known in an insidious way. If our health insurance were to become compulsory, it is easy to see how these defects might multiply and actually jeopardize the health of the nation.

A system of socialized medicine tends to weaken one's reasons for being well. A struggle for livelihood is no longer required. If a leg is broken, the state pays medical, hospital, and operation costs, and advances adequate funds for living until the bone is healed. But there is the rub. If a man suffers no material disadvantage from sickness, there is no material incentive for him to recover rapidly. But if loss of income goes with the broken leg, he will be anxious to have it heal so that he can get back to work as soon as possible. And doubly so, if he pays his own hospital and surgical bills. Doctors know that a broken leg heals very slowly in a welfare state. And for the same reason, the recovery of most patients "protected financially" by insurance companies proceeds slowly and painfully.

Mrs. A and Mrs. B underwent operations for benign fibroid tumors of the uterus on the same day; they were in the same semi-private room, were about the same age, and had almost identical operative procedures. But from the very first postoperative day, any similarity between the two women ended abruptly. Mrs. A recovered rapidly and was eager to get home to her family and her work. Mrs. B seemed to revel in her long recovery because her husband had told her the whole thing was covered by insurance and she should stay in the hospital as long as she wanted. "Don't let them send you home too soon," he said.

Mrs. A went home on her sixth postoperative day, which was routine for her operation; but Mrs. B complained and stayed four days longer, until she "was good and ready." Though her bill was much higher than Mrs. A's, the insurance company paid for all but a few extras.

A routine office visit one month later revealed that Mrs. A had been doing her house work and other chores for almost a week. Mrs. B was not able to climb stairs and had attempted no work beyond drying some dishes the previous day. The prolongation of her recovery, in my opinion, must be attributed to insurance coverage.

There are many examples of comparative amputees, showing that the one obliged to pay his own bill and earn a living recovers faster and learns to use a prosthetic device earlier than the one who is waiting for an insurance settlement. This sort of thing happens far too often to be pure coincidence.

An individual can become ill by just imagining he is ill, or he may be a malingerer from the very beginning. The psychiatrist will tell you that the incentive for either is the thought of increased recompense for being ill. At any rate such persons manage to bring misery upon themselves and to all about them.

Socialized medicine includes government care of the sick and support for the family as well. If this support amounts to approximately the same as the man can earn from his own daily labor, he is tempted to be sick continuously. The temptation would be the greatest for people in low income brackets, illness actually being preferable to good health. This may sound strange, but doctors can observe the fact in their daily practice. Many people want to be sick, or sicker than they actually are, because material advantages in the form of compensations and liability payments are involved.

In accident cases where the recovery period is unusually long, the question of insurance liability and possible future litigation is likely to be present. When referring to the man who has been limping unnecessarily for several months, doctors sometimes jokingly say that John has nothing the matter with him that a prompt and substantial settlement wouldn't cure. But it occurs too often that it is less joke than reality. *Patients who are waiting eagerly and selfishly for the settlement of their claim recover slowly in spite of all treatment.* And usually their complete recovery coincides with the final settlement of the claim. It is easy to see why there are so many cases for the compensation lawyers, referees, and juries. Just imagine the job of sorting all of these malingerers from the truly needy if socialized medicine were available!

The advocates of government in medicine point to our overcrowded hospitals as though they have in mind a solution for the problem. But the fact is that much overcrowding is traceable to increased voluntary insurance benefits, a situation that would only be aggravated if all beds were "free." The waiting lists for the hospitals of England and Germany are so long that many patients finally gain admittance only to have forgotten why they applied.

The hue and cry of overcrowded hospitals is a twisted statistic, for the beds are overburdened with people who are not really sick. The third party in the form of health insurance has entered the picture. But the present sad picture, with only part of our population voluntarily insured, would surely be magnified if health insurance coverage were made universal and compulsory.

Experience with socialized medicine shows hospitals so overcrowded that the situation becomes nearly impossible, doctors so overworked that their patients get less and less real treatment, the cost of drugs reaching astronomical figures, the total cost of the social system soaring, and the government call for investigations. The doctors are accused of high-handed methods, the druggists are accused of charging too much for the pills, the people themselves are accused of being too sick. So finally, more and more there creeps into the picture police controls—"the last refuge of self-bankrupting, socialist planning."[1]

With the obvious increase in the number of insured persons who are demanding medical care and hospitalization, a "doctor shortage" becomes more or less inevitable. Doctors are overwhelmed with the demands of people who feel that their insurance is wasted if they don't use it. Minor and even imaginary ills demand immediate attention. If doctors would only confine their attention to patients who are really ill, the present quota of doctors should have ample time for leisure. If there were the same insurance coverage for plumbing services as for health and accidents, I am convinced that there would be a plumber shortage before the signatures were dry on the policies.

Socialized medicine tends to overwork and tire doctors until they lose interest in the welfare of their patients and are no longer inspired by their original dedication to ideals. When this situation arises, there may be some patients who never get to see their doctors and finally recover because they have no recourse. This leads some persons to ask: "If this condition persists, will not socialized medicine, at least in part, cure some of its own ills?" There may be some merit to this idea on the surface, but when we digest it, we find that it involves quite an expensive cure for people who would get well without help. At the same time, some would die for lack of treatment and others would suffer for lack of the medicine they need. So the self-correcting features of socialized medicine are really no excuse for its adoption. Under our present system, most patients may call one or more of several doctors in their community; but the "beneficiary" of socialized medicine waits for the doctor to whom he has been assigned.

Why Doctors Prefer Freedom

There are many reasons why doctors cry out against socialized medicine. First, as individuals, they abhor the regimentation which is inevitable under socialism. Second, they feel that initiative, research, and humane care of the ill will gradually be replaced by robot dispensing, complacency, and the treatment of a number rather than a human being. Third, they have always thought that giving inferior drugs to increase their profit, or performing less than their best because the pay was predetermined was beneath their professional dignity. All of these shortcomings exist in all of the presently functioning systems of socialized medicine.

If the loss of the hardy physical and mental attributes of the pioneer—to make of us weak and dependent wards of the state—is an incurable disease, then our fate is inevitable. If our youth are to be deprived of the incentive to dedicate their lives to the healing art, and devote their years to learning their profession, then our diseases will be treated by automatons and our health will deteriorate. If the important work of doctors, nurses, technicians, and allied skills is to be minimized and even denied by political charlatans, then these same youths will refuse to enter this noblest of professions except by edict. If we eventually accept all of these proven evils as a system of government and a way of life, then we can blame ourselves for inferior physical and mental health and weak protoplasm. To maintain our health and strength, we had best insist on our present high quality of training, zealous research, and devotion to the prevention and cure of diseases of body and of mind.

---

1. Mechior Palyi, "How Sick is Socialized Medicine?" in *The Freeman*, June 1952.

Socialized Medicine

by Dan Smoot

In 1884, Prince Otto von Bismarck, Chancellor of Germany, instituted the first modern program of socialized medicine. It was called compulsory national health insurance.

Bismarck hated Communism. His motive in introducing socialized medicine in Germany was to buy the loyalty of the German masses as a means of keeping them from becoming Communists. Bismarck adopted "nationalistic socialism to end international socialism"—to use his own words. To use other words: Bismarck was the first leader of a great nation to fight Communism by adopting Communism.

The German citizens paid more for their national compulsory health insurance than they had paid for private insurance before Bismarck came along—and they got less in return.

Bismarck's scheme failed miserably to provide better medical care for the people of Germany; but it did become an important feature of the German militaristic state; it helped pave the way for Hitler a generation later; and it furnished a pattern with which practically every other nation in the West—including America—has experienced.

British Experience

England first started experimenting with socialized medicine in 1911. The experiments were a failure, as they always have been everywhere.

But government never retrenches. When government seizes power and money from the people in order to promote their welfare and then makes matters worse for them, government always argues that it didn't have enough power and money to do enough promoting.

In England, for example, when Lloyd George's rather moderate

Dan Smoot is editor and publisher of *The Dan Smoot Report*. This article appeared in the April 1960 *Freeman*.

experiment in the Bismarckian type of national health insurance was abandoned, the nation went all the way into communized medicine.

The National Health Program which became the law of England in July 1948 is modeled on the Soviet system created by Lenin.

In less than two years, there were more than half a million people on the waiting lists for hospitalization, while some 40,000 hospital beds were out of service because of a nurse shortage. The hospital shortage in Britain has become so acute that many mentally deficient and helpless, aged people are unable to secure institutional care. The only effective means of easing the shortage is to deny hospital admission to the old and chronically ill who cannot be discharged once they are admitted.

In industrial centers, some British doctors have as many as 4,000 registered patients each. Such doctors can give each patient only three minutes per call—three minutes overall, for consultation, diagnosis, prescription, filling out official forms, and maintaining proper records for governmental inspectors.

Twelve percent of all British taxes go into the national health program. Thus the wretchedly inadequate "free" medical services in Britain actually cost the average Englishman considerably more than an American pays for the most expensive private health insurance and hospitalization plan.

Over and above what the British themselves have put into socialized medicine, one must consider also the billions of dollars which America has pumped into the British economy as loans and outright gifts. And still the thing is a failure. Why?

Whenever government enters a field of private activity, that field becomes a political battleground. Whenever you mix politics with medicine, doctoring becomes a political instead of a medical activity.

"Something for Nothing"

But the primary reasons for the inevitable failure of socialized medicine can be found in the patients themselves. When people are forced to pay for something, whether they want it or not, they are inclined to use as much of it as they can in an effort to get their money's worth.

There are endless stories about Englishmen who trade their government-issued eyeglasses, wigs, and even false teeth, for beer. There are housewives who trade government-issued medicine for perfume and cigarettes. And there are some who pick up extra money by selling the gold fillings out of their teeth—getting them replaced by government dentists and then selling them again.

Malingerers are people who pretend to be sick in order to get sick-pay, Social Security benefits, free hospitalization, or a rest at government expense. Hypochondriacs are people who think they are sick, but aren't. There are countless thousands of such people. No system has even been devised for definitely identifying them, for weeding out the unnecessary or unreasonable or dishonest demands made upon the medical care services—no system, that is, except the one existing in a free society where a person must pay his own doctor bill or is controlled by provisions of an insurance policy which he himself has bought.

No compulsory health insurance program has found a means to discourage racketeers or petty complainers who make useless trips to the doctor and monopolize professional time that should be spent on people really needing care.

The Price of Free Medicine

by Colm Brogan

Last year the British National Health Service paid one million pounds ($2,800,000) for bottles and other containers to be used for drugs and medicine. In contrast, the grant for research in mental health was a mere 27 thousand pounds ($75,600).

These figures illustrate the most damaging though least heeded effect of socialized medicine. Floods of money feed the insatiable appetite for pills, while fundamental medical research is largely neglected. Intelligent doctors are fully aware of this threat to the whole future of British medicine, but the British people generally do not sense the danger. Socialized medicine allows popular demand to dictate the use of available resources through political pressure, the consequence being this gross distortion of the strategy and tactics of medical development.

Not even Mr. Bevan himself denies that the British people are heavily overindulging in nostrums of dubious value. Faith in these nostrums is scarcely more intelligent than faith in magic, but vast sums are poured out of the public purse for cures of largely imaginary value for diseases which are also largely imaginary.

At the same time, nearly half the hospital beds in Britain are occupied by mental patients, and many would-be voluntary patients must be refused admission. Conditions in some of these mental hospitals are deplorable. They are badly understaffed and shockingly overcrowded. Yet not one new mental hospital has been opened in Britain since the start of the Health Service, nearly eight years ago. In fact, no hospital of any kind has been built and opened.

At a time when both medical advance and the challenge to medicine are undergoing great and dramatic changes, British practice is being fossilized in attitudes as out of date as the hansom cab and the wooden stethoscope.

Mr. Brogan, a British journalist and author, wrote this article for the June 1956 issue of *The Freeman*.

"Noble Experiment"

That, of course, was not the original purpose of those who framed the Health Act. They offered it as an "experiment noble in purpose"; and the British people were promised everything, regardless of expense. Not only would their home treatments be provided free of direct charge, but the hospitals would for the first time have ample funds for treatment and research. It was said to be a disgrace to a progressive country that the great voluntary hospitals, some of them of world-wide fame, should be dependent on uncertain charity and sorely handicapped in their beneficent work. There would no longer be any need for humiliating appeals, nor restrictions on staffing, building, or research; and in addition, health centers would be established everywhere to bring all the general practitioners of an area together in happy comradeship, with all the most expensive resources of modern medicine at their immediate command.

That was a fine dream, but the reality proved to be far different. The administrators soon found themselves faced with two inescapable facts. The available supply of trained doctors, nurses, and medical scientists, and members of the semiprofessional ancillaries like physiotherapists and speech therapists was not enough to meet all the needs of the grandiose plan.

The financing of the plan was even more strictly limited. Enthusiasts for nationalized medicine found themselves in competition with the enthusiasts for extended education, state-subsidized housing, higher state pensions and benefits, and a dozen other schemes with a strong emotional and vote-catching appeal. There was competition not only for funds, but also for materials and for future staff. While hospital wards were shut for lack of nurses, the potential nurses of the future were tempted into teaching to meet the demands of the rising birth rate and the extra compulsory year at school ordained by the socialist government. Building materials and labor that might have been used for temporary hospital and clinic accommodations were used for temporary classrooms.

If no checks had been put on Health Service expenditure, it would have assumed fantastic proportions. But when expenses soon came to more than double the original estimate, it was found necessary even for a socialist government to impose a ceiling and eventually call a halt.

A part of the corrective action attracted much attention and stirred a good deal of resentment. The patient looking for spectacles or for dental treatment had to pay a proportion of the cost, and for some the proportion was substantial. In addition, all patients were required to pay a shilling for each prescription filled. The prescription charge failed in its purpose, however. Most of the patients resented having to pay and tried to get as much as possible on one prescription, which doubtless encouraged waste. In any event, the Labour Party, which originally imposed the charges, promises to abolish them when they get back to office—a measure of the depths to which demagogy can sink.

Dentists in Difficulty

But the other thing that was done attracted little notice outside of the medical profession. Dentists were paid by piecework, and the original rates for the various jobs were lavishly set to coax dentists into the scheme. For some time, dentists were in financial clover. But the rates have been slashed three times, reducing dentists to a very modest standard and putting some in grim financial difficulty as they must pay surtax on the high earnings of a previous year out of a current income drastically reduced by arbitrary decree. This situation has brought a catastrophically reduced enrollment in dental colleges, thus ending most dreams of a dental service that would concentrate on scientific conservation instead of hasty pulling and patching.

The doctors fared better than the dentists. Their resistance to the scheme had been so strong that they were offered an income equal in purchasing power to the average medical income of 1938. When R. A. Butler became Tory Chancellor of the Exchequer, he was faced with an arbitration award which gave general practitioners not only an increased annual payment for each patient but also a lump sum of fifty million pounds to make up for past underpayment. Nurses and lay hospital workers were in no mood for cuts in salaries and wages. Inflation steadily increased the bill for all hospital supplies and also for the drugs and pills doled out so lavishly through the doctors' offices.

The End of Medical Progress

Thus, the National Health Service budget was strained to the breaking point. And the cuts fell on the unprotected sector of health expenditure, though this was the sector which alone could keep Britain abreast of the civilized world in medical advance. The grandiose schemes of expansion were almost all dropped, and the great teaching and research hospitals suddenly found themselves more pinched than they had ever been before. One hospital, which had almost completed an ambitious and modern laboratory, had to turn the key in the lock for a considerable time because they lacked funds for the microscopes needed if the laboratory were to serve its purpose.

This is only one example of a deleterious process. Public demand and demagogic compliance have diverted available funds away from the fruitful and imperative lines of medical advance in order to supply that kind of medicine which satisfies the credulous patient. The mass of the public were well enough pleased. Hypochondriacs and people with nothing much to do could still crowd a harassed doctor's office at no immediate cost to themselves and call for a pill or a bottle which they might have seen advertised. Many doctors have told me that since the enactment of the Health Act a growing number of patients come to the office and say they want this drug or that, not waiting for the doctor's examination and verdict, but making their own selection as they might choose sweets in a confectioner's shop.

There is the case of a woman whose baby was suffering diaper rash. She got a doctor's prescription for no fewer than ten bottles of an expensive new medication. The rash finally was cured when the woman was told to keep her baby dry and to apply a simple ointment. The ointment which did the trick cost fourpence (about 5 cents); the ten bottles which did no good cost thirty pounds ($84). This is one example of waste, but it could be multiplied indefinitely.

The Ministry of Health has tried to deter doctors from easily prescribing expensive proprietary drugs when much cheaper equivalents are available, but the doctors resent any dictation and the patients are even more resentful.

For a long time it has been the ambition of conscientious practitioners to wean their patients away from this pathetic faith in bottles and pills; but the Health Service has undone all such effort, and fundamental medical research is the chief sufferer.

The brilliant triumphs of modern medicine have nearly all been won in the laboratory, not at the patient's bedside or in the doctor's office. The weight of medical investment should be in that direction, but in Britain it is being swung in what is strictly the reactionary and obsolete way.

Diseased Minds

As for mental illness, which is the greatest and most disturbing challenge to Western civilization, the treatment and the cure of this menace is only in its infancy. Patient research and investigation covering the whole of social life are necessary, and equally necessary is a huge expenditure to provide the material means of effective treatment here and now. But there are British mental hospitals where the patients' beds are so crowded that it is impossible even to put a locker between them. It is impossible to get anything like enough native-trained nurses, men and women, for any kind of hospital; but at the same time, many experienced and highly qualified nurses are employed in "welfare" work where their skill and knowledge are thrown away.

I have no space to deal with the wastefully expensive tests and treatments to safeguard the doctors against legal action by litigious patients, whose court action is likely to be paid for by the same state that pays for the hospitals.

I believe that the contemporary and scientific conception of medicine cannot flourish fully and firmly where medicine has been socialized. The great medical advance will continue, but there is nothing in prevailing British conditions to encourage the hope that British medicine will play in the future as remarkable and as leading a part in that advance as it has played in the past. This pessimism is not purely personal. It is shared by nearly every doctor I know who is alive to what is going on in international medicine, while stagnation of method is forced upon himself.

Medicine and Citizen

by Max S. Marshall

If trends mean anything, the citizens of the United States soon may be voting on the question of socialized medicine. The outcome of such balloting might well depend on an understanding of four major principles of medical relationships.

Let the first be labeled a *principle of indoctrination*. With the same root as the word "doctor," meaning one who teaches, "indoctrination" has come to signify the installation of a doctrine in the recipient, an imposition; whereas teaching, akin to education, is a leading-out process, a guidance of the individual functioning under his own power.

Physicians and those engaged in related medical professions traditionally have shown a reluctance to teach or indoctrinate their patients. Though health departments have long had bureaus of public health education, these formerly functioned largely as passive distributing centers. A school wanting information on how to brush teeth would be provided with a chart, or a lecturer would be assigned if a women's club wanted to know about vaccines. But the initiative was in the hands of the citizens. News articles about medicine used to be generally regarded as morbid, indecent, impertinent, or unethical. The principle of indoctrination had not yet developed.

More recently, however, a public health bulletin confides, "the more attractive the group is to its members, the greater the influence that the group can exert on its members." This exemplifies a complete change in spirit. The public health man becomes, by his own fiat, the Man Who Knows, and thus his real job is to indoctrinate the populace with this wisdom. Greatly concerned when the populace does not accept his dicta, he wonders in what way his methods of indoctrination

The late Dr. Marshall was Chairman of the Department of Microbiology at the University of California Medical Center. This article originally appeared in *The Freeman*, February 1962.

are inadequate. Bigger and better campaigns are planned, not aimed at education but aimed at victory, the sale of his point.

Medical indoctrination is not limited to public health. At least three other groups of indoctrinators fire at us citizens.

One, the advertisers, are out to sell. Though seldom going outside of medical journals, they resort increasingly to high-pressure appeals. Informing the medical public is a worthy goal, but selling the product has become a greater one.

A second category, the medical writers, vary in their output from excellent—such as Greer Williams' *Virus Hunters,* highly informative, not sensational, and in good balance—to articles which are no more than dramatic shockers or bits of ebullient and misleading optimism. Since medicine to the layman is more emotional than scientific, only the best in medical writing has any place, and even then spots for it are few.

A third group of indoctrinators are the medical men who write for public consumption in the news columns and editorial pages. The world has grown callous to such ballyhoo and the dangers of a little knowledge. Because medicine is complex, an unprepared mind cannot put in its place a brief comment in lay terms. Try to consider hemorrhage as a topic and keep out of trouble: internal, external, sign of disease, minor traumata, surgical, risks of infection, clotting, hemophilia—even to a layman the list of complexities mounts rapidly. Hypochondriacs may enjoy wallowing in morbidity, but there is no need to force it upon all of us.

The principle of indoctrination in medical knowledge, even in a sense of teaching, has little to support it; but the trend is toward more and more of it.

Compulsory Participation

The second principle, allied in thought to indoctrination, is the *principle of compulsory participation.* To what extent can, should, or does an organized medical interest impose itself on citizens by legal force? This question arises in matters of compulsory medical insurance, compulsory vaccination, school legislation, and even in the clinic.

In the clinic, however, the feeling of compulsion is minimal. No one forces the patients who go past my window to come into the clinic. They are examined and perhaps an operation seems wise; but it is suggested, not demanded. Patients may be told to come back in a week, but not all do; and no one sends a policeman after them. Even when a physician tells a patient to stop drinking lest he drop dead, the patient is on his own after the warning.

Compulsion is not part of the language or the way of life of trained physicians. In public health, however, are to be found all sorts of born missionaries, compulsive thinkers.

"The new state law requiring compulsory polio shots for school children will not go into effect until...." says a recent news item. The matter is of particular interest to me, and I had followed it, but this was my first information that such a law was even being considered. The compulsive thinkers, annoyed at the slow response to their publicized campaigns, had moved very quietly to the legislative halls. Instead of raising the question to find the truth, their goal is to convince the legislators that they, the proponents, are right in knowing what is good for all of us.

In this instance, one of the most open questions about the use of polio vaccine is the effect it has on the distribution of the virus of poliomyelitis. The inactivated vaccine is generally known to be ineffective in stopping the distribution, yet some communities have barred unvaccinated children from public schools. This is bigotry, not medicine.

The live vaccine operates differently and in theory might block some distribution of the virus (it will not stamp out the disease), but it also offers new risks. Its effect on a whole population cannot be known for some years because polio, despite all the advertising, is still relatively uncommon. Its outbreaks or ups and downs are notoriously uncertain. Based on the record, the injection of salt solution the year before would seem to have been effective in many years. Is it not odd that the urge to make a vaccine compulsory is so often associated with products which would seem to work successfully, regardless of their value? Consider, for example, that a lump of sugar, backed by a little ritual, would seem to prevent polio 9,999 times out of 10,000 on the average. That is pretty good batting!

As for compulsory insurance, listen to the proponents as they try to play God. They claim, for instance, that some improvident folk will never take out insurance unless they are forced. The implication is that "of course you and I would not be so foolish." Once upon a time a U.S. citizen had a constitutionally respected right to be foolish, and a corresponding duty to abide by the consequences. We are developing a race in which everyone seems slightly annoyed at his own duties. Under this attitude we are ready to save the other fellow's soul at the drop of a hat.

In Whose Jurisdiction?

This brings us to a third category, the *principle of trespass*. One of the oldest debates in the realm of public medicine arose when federal agriculturalists, in charge of food and cows, found themselves embroiled in problems of health over which others claimed jurisdiction. Is the use of weed killers, sprays, preservatives, freezing methods, or milk from tuberculous cows a problem for the Department of Agriculture or for the Department of Health, Education and Welfare? With no absolute answer demonstrable, political jockeying decides the issue.

In medicine the "general practitioner" is in a sort of gentlemanly opposition to the specialists: surgeons, heart specialists, otorhinolaryngologists, ophthalmologists, and so on. But physicians are by no means so sure of the answers as they may seem.

True, distinctions among specialists may rest on profound differences. A surgeon is likely to be a decisive person, a chooser of blacks and whites, whose decisions are as clean as his wounds: The leg may come off or it may not, but it will never come half way off. The general practitioner on the other hand, is likely to be more palliative, gray, less sure, more tolerant to theory, able to feel optimistic about treatments in which cause and effect are almost never clearly related as they are with the surgeon.

But most general practitioners call on specialists quickly when the going gets tough; and most specialists check on background, relating their tasks to the whole patient. In their puzzling and often puzzled relationships with laymen, physicians prefer not to trespass outside their fields even as much as they should.

Again, public health affords a prime exhibit of trespass. Public health education was pedestrian, so it shifted from education to indoctrination. Calling some of its problems essentially solved—safe milk and water, quarantine, marked reduction in tuberculosis, less spectacular epidemics—public health sought other fields of glory.

Does the health official admit that the perfect measure of his progress would be the rate of regression of his staff and duties? Not by a jugful! And so the health official seeks drama and a basis for expansion. He trespasses, grasping everything in medicine which is not tied down.

Property is condemned by a health department, unless the city officials own it—the same health department that moans because agriculture trespasses. Epidemics of measles still occur, but health officials rather scoff at such and talk preferably about the epidemiology of heart disease and cancer, problems strictly in the realm of physicians. They talk about automobile accidents. Schools of public health, engaged in data-collecting—busywork which is always available for rainy days in all walks of life—take over statistics, a mathematical field notably unsafe out of the hands of mathematicians and not always safe then.

Organizational Problems

The fourth principle of operational medicine is the *principle of organization*. Both "rugged individualists" and "organization men" tend to agree that we need (a) some answer to socialized medicine, (b) some outlook which will put hospitals on realistic footing with medical practice, (c) some basis by which medicine can be kept in the hands of those trained instead of being trampled in legislative halls, and (d) some method for policing medicine.

From my ringside seat I have seen, I think, that medical men had pretty well ironed out the sociology of medicine. They are completely baffled by an uprising of a citizenry for which they have been caring, a citizenry which has little if any concept of the medical problems involved.

Hospital bills are astronomical compared to the bills of physicians, for reasons some of which are crystal clear. Hospital insurance, for example, is ungoverned and means that neither doctor nor patients concern themselves with needs and costs. Hospital administration, for another example, is garbled, because most doctors or other superintendents are not trained for hotel management.

As for nonmedical interference, consider New York, 1947. A man with smallpox came to town and went through streets, subways, stores, and hospital waiting rooms and wards. In the course of two months a dozen cases occurred; the first case and his wife died. A huge campaign led to some 6,000,000 vaccinations in a few weeks. Only a few men claimed to know what was good for everyone; but the campaign was ruled by the Mayor, columnists, radio broadcasters, professional publicists who were weak in medicine, strong in causes and indoctrinations. The small outbreak, hardly deserving that name, killed fewer persons than the literally countless vaccinations. Several hundred vaccinations, if that many, would have restrained the spread (what spread?) of the disease, because this was 1947 and a high percentage of the population had had vaccine. The situation supported the normal vaccinating program; it was against hysteria. After spending seven to twelve years in training, on top of whatever years have been added by experience, a physician in cases of public hysteria is literally not allowed to use his best medical judgment, the thing for which he is trained and paid. To his own mental tortures raised by the medical problem are added those unbearable additional ones which society imposes.

Policing of medicine has been tackled occasionally by the only proper policemen, the medical fraternity itself. Among 170,000 persons in any field, problems of discipline and policing are bound to arise. The rare medical groups which acknowledge this and attempt to do their own policing are very quiet; but the best police work is usually done quietly.

A noteworthy point about medical practice is that patients do not have to inquire of Flunky A, who asks Manager B, who consults Vice President C, who phones to President D, who puts the question up to the Board of Directors. The patient gets to see the doctor, in person. This is the essence of medical practice, and it is significant.

Clearly, most physicians are not interested in organizational headaches. I have faced over two thousand future M.D.'s in my classes and have seen many physicians in action. Almost to a man they are bored stiff by meetings of committees. When they join in debates, they usually go directly to the issue. In their offices the patient, the physician, and the disease are paramount; neither person is interested in extraneous rituals. If doctors are not interested in the migraine brought on by emphasis on organization, can they be forced to function in it? I think not, successfully. They ignore it or rise above it, and go to a patient somewhere and talk about *his* migraine.

The generalization that physicians are mercenaries is improper. Some of them make big incomes. Now and then one of them fails to report all to the Internal Revenue officer, not necessarily deliberately, for income taxes require organization. Even as students a few of them indicate that they will seek country club practices and deal with patients with incidental chronic diseases, which bring in steady large incomes with no worries. But, as a group, a good case cannot be made that physicians are mercenaries.

Beyond the shadow of doubt, their minds are filled with medical problems most of the time. With certainty it can be said that most of them work long and odd hours, with rare vacations; being mercenary serves no purpose. The responsibilities they take, their relatively availability, their period of training, their freedom of operation, the overhead carried in an office, the cost of equipment, their small but necessary payroll, all suggest that a substantial income is earned.

The Great Questions

With the two great questions, the status of public health and the status of socialized medicine, even with risks incidental to oversimplification, conclusions seem conspicuous.

Public health, as it stands today, is highly organizational, and physicians stand away. Their patients are persons rather than populations. Public health as now managed calls for publicity, also anathema to physicians. It involves politics, still less desired. It calls for mass moves and compulsion, of debatable merit. Whereas public health originally stood for clean restaurants, understandable to and tolerated by physicians, it has come to be a sort of maelstrom of unpredictable propaganda, not understandable at all.

Thus physicians do not understand public health folks, and *vice versa*. Several years ago a pharmaceutical house discovered that, by advancing a product through public health instead of through the usual medical channel, they got free advertising and mass moves. Whereas public health stampeded prematurely for polio vaccine, physicians then were saying quietly that they would like a few answers yet before giving it to their patients and families.

Public health might conceivably be better off in the hands of physicians. Citizens could then perhaps pay for it, a prospect which seems so unlikely under policies of unlimited expansion. Matters which are strictly medical would then have no interference from public health. Matters which are not medical in any way would be dropped or appropriately delegated. This suggestion, though radical, is not impossible. Public health is essentially a community affair, not a state or federal matter. Doctors and patients intrinsically are of the community.

As for socialized medicine, today's compulsory approach is destroying the very practical and effective alternative we once enjoyed. The amount of wearing effort or expensive time given away by physicians was colossal and is still significant.

Examine the effect of "socialized medicine" on the hypochondriacs who clutter up "free clinics" until physicians find ways to block them off; or weigh the best service of a physician who must sit up until midnight bookkeeping instead of studying medicine, seeing a patient, or even relaxing like other folk. Compare civil service employees as a socially bound class with those of a live organization, and then think of physicians as rule-bound employees instead of as independent highly trained detectives on whom we depend for our lives. Weigh the rights of both patients and physicians and the degree to which they are stymied by organizational maneuvers.

Without excessive organization and without noise, fuss, or feathers, physicians were doing fairly well until an untrained citizenry pointed its guns at them. So long as we have good physicians they will continue to smile and remain aloof in silence. When and if we should shift to mere trained technicians and slaves of the state, medical efficiency would suffer basically for lack of the finest of all ingredients, the quality of those persons in the profession. The threat is already showing its effects. The men and women of medicine inevitably make it what it is. Give them latitude and they will catch up with some criticisms; and we citizens may learn that many of our comments are uninformed and narrow, invalid.

Medical men and women, human and subject to the slings and arrows of the same fortunes that greet us, are the absolute best that we have to meet the physical woes which have to be met. They will remain our best bet so long as they are allowed the independence and dignity of a profession which, be it called noble or morbid, is one of our greatest needs.

Why Deny Health Care?

by Robert K. Oldham, M.D.

Most Americans would agree that "health care should be available equally to everyone." But now the thesis of equal availability of health care is beginning to translate into a sub-thesis: "If everyone can't have a health-care service, then no one should have it."

Recent medical advances have made available a variety of in-depth approaches to the treatment of serious disorders such as cancer, AIDS, and major organ failure that allow for correction, or a research-based attempt at correction, of the disorder. Transplantation brings forth a large number of potential recipients, a small number of donors, and huge costs for each kidney, heart, or liver transplant. These transplant stories are often in the news and may involve distressing reports of the need for a transplant in a child, a young mother, or a productive, breadwinner father.

The relative infrequency of the transplant dilemma has been a major saving grace. Our sympathies go to each patient, and many of us have contributed to help a scientific patient. No effective system-wide solution to the limited availability of this expensive technology has come forth.

Individuals who can afford to pay for these transplants represent a major revenue stream for hospitals with transplant services. There is little discussion when the individual has the capability to pay for a transplant. Is it not a wonder that the issue of restricting availability to those who can afford the transplant hasn't been raised by ethicists? There has been broad negative reaction to the idea of "selling" organs, but transplant programs go forward when organs are available for individuals who can pay for the procedure.

More difficult is the issue of a new cancer treatment or a new

---

Dr. Oldham is Chairman and Scientific Director of Biotherapeutics, Inc., based in Franklin, Tennessee, a firm which conducts cancer research for patients in the private sector. This article first appeared in the March 1989 *Freeman*.

approach to the devastating problem of AIDS. In both of these situations, there has been much discussion about access and opportunity, the cost of research and medical services, and the issue of availability. Government and university officials have often voiced the view that a certain number of research-based approaches should be available through their hospitals. Individuals should line up and wait for the opportunity to avail themselves of these research services.

Such a system resembles the National Health Service of Britain, except that in the United States, contacts, political pressure, and money often can abridge a system of equal opportunity for all. One is reminded of kidney dialysis in its early days—an expensive technology for which committees were created to judge the worthiness of individuals in need. In spite of such committees, patients with resources were generally able to avail themselves of dialysis.

Once rejected from such a system or once on a too-long waiting list with too little time, why restrain an individual with resources from pursuing private options? It would seem obvious that an individual with resources should be able to use those resources as he or she sees fit, while alive and able to make rational decisions. Yet, there is an increasing call to restrain such individuals from pursuing private-sector opportunities to gain access to new medical technologies for the treatment of cancer or AIDS.

The arguments go something like this: "If a medical service isn't available for everyone, should it be available for a few? Isn't it unethical or morally repugnant for someone with assets to be able to pursue a new, research-based treatment approach when others, without these resources, cannot? Shouldn't there be restraints on the private sector in the delivery of medical services to those who wish to pay for them?"

This thought process would indeed be bizarre if it were applied to a vital product such as food. At the moment, no one is crying foul if someone with resources chooses to eat more than the minimum daily requirement. In a similar manner, there has been no call to restrict the availability of air conditioners for those who wish to purchase them in spite of the obvious health advantages of air conditioning to the sick and elderly who can't afford them. There has been no call to remove private rooms or executive suites from hospitals where they are available to patients with resources. There has been no call to restrain travel by those who wish to fly to Switzerland or Italy or to a distant clinical facility within the United States for specialized medical care.

Different Standards of Ethics?

As a physician, I often receive calls from individuals who ask if I have access to a specialized technology, a research-based approach, for the treatment of a relative. I am struck by the fact that the individual, often a practicing physician, has not called me about his patients. I am struck that such individuals often work in government or universities. Some have been openly critical of private-sector systems of cancer research that might provide opportunities for those with the resources to afford them—until someone close needs access and opportunity. What are the ethics of one standard for a relative and a different approach for a patient? This curious schizophrenia between the idea that everyone should have equal access, but that if everyone can't have it, no one should, represents a dangerous thought process.

To translate that to a system where no one can have access to more health care beyond a set standard would be a grievous error. Such thinking outside of the health field is clearly anomalous. Let's not apply a unique standard to health-care services, but let's apply the same rules of logic to all basic services that individuals might use, given their resources.

"Third Party" Medicine

by James L. Doenges, M.D.

No ethical physician would claim that he healed the patient's wounds or made the patient well. None can do more than assist the natural processes. If the physician were the final authority, every patient would recover quickly and none would die. No physician can fail to realize his personal limitations. He must admit the existence of a Greater Power. No other profession renders services in this intimate area in which the individual faces life and death. This brings the physician into a more intimate relationship with the patient than exists between the same individual and any other professional person. Complete mutual understanding and confidence is essential and seldom exists outside this area of intimate contact.

The best interest of the patient requires that the individual patient-physician relationship be held inviolate in every area. This includes every contact between the patient and his physician, whether it involves the history, examination, and treatment, or the area of compensation for services.

Highest quality medical care cannot exist if the traditional moral and ethical concepts of medical practice are violated. The key to good diagnosis is a good, honest, and complete history. The knowledge that information confided to the physician will not be divulged to others permits even the most timid patient to give the most personal, intimate, and confidential information to his physician. Consultants are frequently denied this same information which is freely given to the patient's "own" doctor.

For thousands of years physicians have fought for the right to hold inviolate from all probers and other curious individuals facts elicited in the medical history and examination. These rights of privileged

---

The late Dr. Doenges, past president of the Association of American Physicians and Surgeons, was a surgeon in Anderson, Indiana. This article appeared in the August 1959 *Freeman*.

communication, granted and enforced by courts of justice, are essential for successful treatment.

In the final analysis only two individuals are involved in medical care: the patient, who has chosen the physician to whom he will entrust his care and actually his life, and his physician, who has freely agreed to provide such care. (Due consideration is given to those individuals for whom another acts "in loco parentis.") No other person, no "third party,"[1] is required. When any third party enters the picture, he is an intruder and can only reduce the uninhibited rapport and confidence which must exist between patient and physician.

Nongovernmental Bureaucracy

All are acquainted with the numerous difficulties and objections reported regarding the operation of third party national health insurance schemes, such as the "red tape," the innumerable forms which require more time than the patient receives, the sky-rocketing costs with the associated tax increases, the increasing demands for nonessential services and supplies, the abuses which defy elimination, the ever-increasing waiting lists for hospital admissions, the unreasonable delays in every area, the decreasing hospital services, the dissatisfaction among patients, hospital personnel, and physicians, as well as the wasteful operation and other evils to which every bureaucracy is heir. Bureaucratic systems are not confined to governmental agencies. They can and do exist in most businesses, labor unions, and some medical organizations.

These facts alone provide sufficient concrete reasons why government, and other Third Party health programs via insurance or service plans, historically result in less satisfactory and inferior quality medical care.

Quality of Service Suffers

However, there are other and more important factors which make it impossible for medical care supplied through third party programs to equal or even approach the quality of medical care supplied through private practice operating under the market economy.

An essential feature of quality medical practice is that the patient is and must be regarded as an individual—a moral being. Individuality is the very basis of the practice of medicine. All medical tradition emphasizes the fact that every patient is an individual, that his ills are singular, and that he must be so regarded and treated. Health and disease are strictly personal matters.

Personal responsibility, upon which all freedom depends, is another basic essential in the successful practice of medicine. It applies to the patient as well as to the physician.

The patient's responsibility cannot be eliminated or violated. If he withholds information or misrepresents facts to his physician, he removes one of the basic requirements for good care. He ties the physician's hands. If the physician does not share the confidence of his patient, he cannot treat the patient adequately or properly and his chances of helping are greatly reduced. If the physician disregards the facts, the patient suffers. Medical care is not a mechanical function!

How Choice Is Limited

Third-party medical care always results in control of the patient and the physician by limiting the free choice of the patient in selecting his physician and by interfering with the individual patient-physician relationship. Physicians are frequently classified, not according to ability, but on an arbitrary and unrealistic basis such as membership in certain organizations or other interesting but relatively unimportant details. Experience, results, ability, confidence of patients, and personal interest are relegated to a minor position. Physicians are rated by third-party agencies as to the type of practice they may perform and the type of disorder they may treat.

Freedom of choice is further limited because the services which may be rendered by any classification are controlled and regulated by the third party.

Under third party control, physicians are paid according to classification regardless of whether it is on a fee for services, per capita, panel, hourly, or salary basis. All third party programs eventually utilize the principle of fixed fees.

Physicians who participate in such schemes must agree to render totally unknown and unpredictable quantities of service for a predetermined fee. The taxpayer is promised by politicians or third-party officials that physicians will deliver any and all services for a fee set by the third party. In the final analysis, the third party always establishes the fee to *its* satisfaction! This procedure inevitably and obviously places the emphasis on the quantity of medical care and relegates quality to a position of secondary importance.

No One Is Responsible

Under any system of third party medical programs the patient must accept the "third party" into the patient-physician relationship in every area, not in the area of fees alone.

The physician is required to accept the third party by reporting or certifying illness to someone other than the patient himself. This begins the deterioration of and destruction of the confidential nature of the patient-physician relationship.

The patient feels justified in relinquishing his responsibility in return for the third party's payment of fees. The physician also begins to look to the third party in this area of responsibility and justifies his attitude by the requirement of supplying the third party with information. The physician even begins to hold the third party responsible for what he regards as the proper use of the funds removed from the patient not infrequently by force, by dues, royalties, taxes, or other means.

These practices encourage the patient to divorce himself from his sense of personal responsibility to his physician in the area of fees. Having accepted the idea that someone else may rightly assume his responsibility, it becomes a matter of indifference to the patient, and eventually to the physician, who assumes this responsibility.

At the point where the physician accepts such an agreement, he joins his patient in flight from personal responsibility and accepts the idea that a third party is responsible for the payment of the patient's bills, and in so doing, grants to the third party the right to establish his fees and the category in which he may function.

Destroying the Market Economy

The attempt to establish third-party medical programs is a definite attempt to destroy the market economy.

Any argument in favor of third-party medical programs may be used, by changing a few words, with equal validity to promote third-party control of every other profession; every other need and desire; in short, of every segment of the economy.

Highest quality medical care cannot survive under any system in which there is third-party interference. This has been and will be true, always, regardless of the promises of politicians or businessmen, the misrepresentations of labor union leaders, or the compromises of some in the medical profession.

Remember one thing: *Only doctors can deliver medical services. Only individuals trained and experienced in the healing arts can fill the medical needs of the people of this nation.*

Our obligation and responsibility is to the individual patient. All agreements must be with each individual patient!

We should never refuse to deliver services to our patients but those services should be delivered to individuals as our own private patients, not as wards of the government, a union, any insurance company, or any other third party.

---

1. For the purpose of this discussion, the "third party" is defined as: any individual, agent, or agency, through whose control of persons or control and/or administration of funds belonging to or assignable to the patient (or for his care), occupies a position capable of affecting the patient's choice of a physician to provide medical care for himself and others for whose care he is legally and/or morally responsible, or of affecting the freedom of the unrestricted bilateral patient-physician relationship.

This discussion does not include consideration of those special cases such as individuals in prisons, in military service, and the like, and the very special situation wherein industry is required by law to assume the position of "parent" in cases under workman's compensation laws.

Health Care: Cross Questions
and Crooked Answers

by Clarence B. Carson

At the sometimes innocent parties I went to when I was an adolescent we occasionally played a game called "Cross Questions and Crooked Answers." Boys were lined up on one side and girls on the other. Each boy was handed a slip of paper on which a question was written. Each girl got one with an answer. When they had been written, each question had an appropriate answer to it. But they were passed out randomly so that the questions no longer matched the answers when they were read. If all went well, there would be a series of malapropisms, inanities, and ribaldries.

A variation of Cross Questions and Crooked Answers has now achieved adult status. Political involvement in medicine has made it commonplace without our being aware of it. Let us take a statement first. It is usually worded something like this: "Every American should have quality medical care." Now, the question, "Don't you want the best quality medical care possible?" It is tempting to treat this as a straight question, and to make what appears to be the only reasonable answer. Namely, "Of course, I want the best quality medical care possible." From that point on the discussion degenerates into a debate as to which is the best possible system for providing quality medical care. It may not be a futile debate, but it is apt to be inconclusive because the best points have been conceded by the answer given to the question.

This is so because "Don't you want the best medical care possible?" is a Cross Question. It is a Cross Question which will most likely elicit a Crooked Answer. Indeed, it is what one of my professors in graduate school called a false question. A false question is one which

---

Clarence B. Carson, Ph.D., has written and taught extensively, specializing in American intellectual history. His most recent book is *Basic Government*. This article originally appeared in the May 1980 issue of *The Freeman*.

147

can only be answered by giving an answer that will be in some part wrong, regardless of what angle you take on it.

To illustrate, let me give the opposite answer to the question, a somewhat perverse answer, if you like. "No, I do not want the best possible medical care. In fact, I do not *want* medical care at all. Medical care is not something one drools over, like a steak, the best cut of which everyone should have. I do not long for the ministrations of physicians or for the comforts of a hospital bed. Indeed, my preferences run in the opposite direction, to have as little truck with any of these as possible."

The answer is evasive, of course, but it is evasion with a point. I want the question reworded. The first order of business is not the quality of medical care; medical care is only a means, not an end. The quality of life is my main concern, not the quality of medical care. The question might be rephrased this way: What do you want from life to which medical care (and its quality presumably) is directly related? Now that is a straight question which can be given a straight answer.

My answer would go something like this. I want the use of my faculties with as little impairment as possible. I want to see, hear, smell, feel, walk, taste, talk, and use my limbs well so that I can function normally. Why? So that I can look after myself. So that I can manage my own affairs. So that I can be independent in order to fulfill my purpose as a man. In short, my concern with medical care is as an adjunct to my personal independence.

Restore the Patient

Contemporary medical practice has this as its primary aim. Its aim is to maintain or restore the independence of the individual, to get him up and walking again, to get him to looking after his bodily needs, to get him to exercising his faculties, and so on. The desired goal is dismissal of the patient and a minimal dependence on drugs. In short, good medical practice requires that the patient be restored to independent status as quickly as in the judgment of the attending physician he is ready for it.

Medical care cannot correctly be considered in a vacuum. When we do so we can only ask Cross Questions and get Crooked Answers about it. It is part of the larger corpus of life itself, and ordinarily a subordinate part. In the context of the statements made above, the aim of medical care—the maintaining and restoring of personal independence—is part of the broader aim of personal independence for individuals. Whatever impairs the independence of the individual will tend to be detrimental to the aims of medicine.

Government intervention is on a collision course with the best in contemporary medical practice. This may be clear to some when the matter is considered only from the angle of quality medical care, but it should be apparent to all when it is looked at from the broader angle of the independence of individuals. The purpose of medicine is to foster individual independence; the impact of government intervention is to reduce the independence of the individual and make him dependent on government. It is this case that is conceded or ignored when we focus exclusively on quality of medical care.

Perpetual Dependence

Here is a story which illustrates how government intervention tends to thwart the broader purpose of medicine by establishing perpetual dependencies. It is a true story. It is even a kind of horror story when its implications are contemplated. Here it is.

Several years ago I was living and working in Pennsylvania. My father lived in Alabama and was, when most of these events transpired, in a small hospital in Georgia. One evening, I got a call from my sister who told me that our father was very ill and that the doctor had said the family should be notified. Presumably, he was dying. It would not have been surprising, for he was 88 years old and had not been in good health for some time.

We flew the next day to see him. Two aspects of his condition stood out. One was that he had lost weight—in fact, was not far from being emaciated. The other was that he had been having hallucinations. He was conscious most of the time, knew everyone, and was lucid enough in conversation. Except, it soon became clear to me that when he was at his best he still believed in the reality of what he had seen when he was hallucinating. I spent the better part of a day at his bedside, and he seemed to want to talk about his hallucinations. (He did not call them that, of course; they were to him unpleasant things he had actually experienced.)

When I talked to the attending physician—in fact, he was the only doctor associated with the hospital—he was rather vague. His prognosis was that my father might die at any time, or he might live for a while longer. Beyond that, he only observed that it was good for me to visit with my father. I began to learn some interesting, and disturbing, things about the hospital, too. It was preternaturally quiet, and they tried to keep it that way. There were few visitors, except those who came to see my father. One did not encounter patients in the hallways, though there were several nurses about. On inquiry, I was told that the patients were all old and bedridden.

In fact, it was not what I would call a hospital; it was a nursing home with a physician and nurses in attendance, and hospital rates were being charged. Whether all the patients were being given tranquilizers, I do not know, but my father was. It was a place where old people on Medicare were brought to die.

A Change for the Better

We moved my father to another hospital as soon as we could get an ambulance. I later talked with the new physician who had examined him there. He indicated that it was too soon to make a firm prognosis but that the vital signs were all good. My father was in no imminent danger, as far as could be determined. I asked if the medication he had been given would be continued. No, the doctor said, for the time, at least, he would be taken off all drugs. What about diet, I asked. My father could eat anything he wanted, he said, and would be encouraged to eat. (He had been on a restricted diet under the other physician.)

The atmosphere in this hospital was quite different from the other one. It was alive. Patients were clearly there only temporarily for healing, and recuperation. I was there once when the physician came in to see my father. He talked to him about going home, about his getting up from the bed, and about going hunting, which was one of my father's favorite activities. Subtly, he was getting my father to think of getting well and inviting him back to life.

Within a day a considerable change had occurred in my father. He was more cheerful; he had begun to eat, and was beginning to do things for himself. Within a short time, he returned home to take up the normal course of his life. He lived for several years after these events, and most of the time he was up and about. The memory of the hallucinations only faded slowly, but otherwise he was better than he had been for some time.

A Cure that Kills

From what illness was my father suffering? It is reasonable to conclude, *ex post facto,* that he was suffering most directly from malnutrition and drug-induced hallucinations. Add to that the fear that arises from helplessness when one suspects he is terminally ill and is waited on hand and foot. The malnutrition was no doubt a consequence of the restricted diet plus an habitual finickiness about eating. There may have been some justification for the restricted diet, for he had arteriosclerosis and complained from time to time of angina attacks, though they were not usually severe. As for the tranquilizers, I can only speculate as to why they were prescribed. Father was inclined to be a noisy patient, groaning and making some loud sound when a pain struck him. The tranquilizers were supposed to keep him quiet, though they did not succeed in doing so.

More broadly, he was a victim of the Dependency Syndrome induced by government involvement in medicine. My father had become dependent on government to pay for at least a portion of his medical care. The physician had become dependent upon government for much, or most, of his income. This arrangement is conducive to the establishing of a relation of continual dependence upon medical care in the patient. For quite a while before my father had been confined in that small hospital he had gone regularly to that physician's office for injections. There was no prospect that he would get well or be dismissed. After each brief session with the physician, he was let go with these words, "See you again in two weeks."

So far as a layman may judge of such matters, that man had earlier been a competent physician. He had been a skilled surgeon with a good practice. I knew him some two decades before the events related above, and at that time he was interested in healing his patients, getting them back on their feet, and dismissing them from his care as soon as the situation warranted it. The eventual independence of his patients was his goal.

In the interval, he had changed. He was no longer practicing medicine. He was practicing Medicare. He had bought the government's line. Government had proclaimed, by its actions, that medical care was a good for the aged. It was a good of such importance that it should be made readily available at the taxpayers' expense. If medical care is such a good, is it not reasonable to conclude that the aged should continually receive it? And there could be no doubt that he was dispensing a considerable amount of medical care, or something that had the look of it.

Too Much Care

But medical care is not a good. It is, if I may so phrase it, a "bad." Drugs can have disastrous side effects. Diets can starve. Lying in bed, even in a hospital, can have debilitating effects. Dependency on doctors, nurses, and medicines is unwholesome. True, a skillful physician, with sound and independent judgment, attentive to the condition of his patients, can use medicine, diets, hospitals, and all the other paraphernalia of modern medical practice to good effect. This tells us, too, what is good: It is the skill, the sound judgment, the independence, and the careful attention. That is the good for which we should pay, and, having had to pay, we are reminded that it is scarce and should be used only when there is some need.

The quality of medical care is a secondary issue. What is at issue primarily in the thrust of government into medicine is individual independence. The great aim of medical practice is *not* to provide medical care; it is to restore patients to whatever status of independence is possible. The best medicine is sometimes no medicine at all. However, that decision should not be made by dispensers of medical care but by medical doctors of *independent* judgment. Government intervention reduces the independence of physicians and of the population generally. A physician may still heal a particular disease, but he cannot restore the full independence of a man who has become deeply dependent on government. The doctor in the small hospital was not on a collision course with government; he had accepted the dependent status of those whom he treated and was bent on perpetuating it.

It is not my purpose here, however, to dismiss the question of quality. Once it has been placed in the broader context to which it belongs—the quality of life—it can be properly considered. No doubt, most people would like to have a high quality of treatment when they stand in need of medical attention. Thus, some observations on the impact of government intervention on the quality of medicine are now in order.

Why Intervention Fails

The tendency of government intervention is to increase the quantity and reduce the quality. It does so for three reasons mainly.

First, by removing or reducing the cost factor in medical treatment, it increases the demand for it. Given the same number of medical personnel, the result is longer waits in doctors' offices, less attention per patient in hospitals, and a dilution of the quality of what is received.

Second, when government prescribes standards of treatment they are, and must be, *minimum* standards. To put it another way, whatever standard government prescribes becomes the *minimum* standard. The way this works was well illustrated in housing. Most houses built over the last thirty or forty years have four inches of insulation above the ceiling. Much of this is blown-in insulation. Why? Because F.H.A. required four inches of insulation, and that is what most houses got. It was widely claimed that the F.H.A. requirements became the standard of the industry. They were, of course, *minimum* (and inadequate) standards, something the rising cost of energy has helped to bring to our attention. (The F.H.A. standard having been discredited did not, of course, lead that organization to retire from the field. It has simply set higher standards which, in turn, have become the *minimum* standard.) A similar development is occurring in the generic drug movement. If the F.D.A. and other agencies are successful, minimally effective drugs will become the standard. To the extent that government pays for medical attention, it will be in accord with minimal requirements. Open-heart surgery with a triple bypass, will be open-heart surgery with a triple bypass, and that is what will be paid for. In short, far from providing the highest quality medical care possible, we will tend to get the lowest quality which the law allows.

Third, government intervention tends to restrain and inhibit innovation. No standards can be set for that which does not exist, and no price scales can be devised. We are experiencing already the slowdown that results from having to gain government approval before new drugs can be put on the market. The testing requirements are already so prohibitive that men will tend to turn their energies away from trying to innovate. The same restrictions do not yet apply to procedures, but there is an inhibitive tendency there also.

The Quality of Life

This brings us back, however, to my original point. The quality of medical treatment cannot be fully considered as separate from the quality of life in general. The innovations which raise the quality of medicine are themselves a product of the independence and freedom of individuals. Reduction in the independence of individuals by restrictions must inevitably result in lower quality medical treatment than would otherwise have been available. But medical treatment itself is but an adjunct to the independence of individuals.

In the final analysis, then, there is one straight question that can be asked which, when it is answered straight, provides the answers to the subordinate questions as well. It is this: Do you want that quality of life which is possible when individuals are independent? If so, you will want as well the availability of the highest quality of medical treatment.

PRICE LIST

The *Freeman Classics* Series

Quantity	Price Each
1 copy	$14.95
2-4 copies	12.00
5-49 copies	9.00
50-499 copies	7.50
500 copies	6.00

Please add $3.00 per order for shipping and handling. Send your order, with accompanying check or money order, to The Foundation for Economic Education, 30 South Broadway, Irvington-on-Hudson, New York 10533. Visa and MasterCard telephone and fax orders are welcome. Call (914) 591-7230 weekdays or fax (914) 591-8910 anytime.

About the Foundation for Economic Education

The Foundation for Economic Education (FEE) is a "home" for the friends of freedom everywhere. Its spirit is uplifting, reassuring, contagious: FEE has inspired the creation of numerous similar organizations at home and abroad.

FEE is the oldest conservative research organization dedicated to the presentation of individual freedom and the private-property order. It was established in 1946 by Leonard E. Read, and guided by its adviser, the eminent Austrian economist, Ludwig von Mises. Both served FEE until their deaths in 1983 and 1973, respectively.

Throughout the years the mission of FEE has remained unchanged: to study the moral and intellectual foundation of a free society and share its knowledge with individuals everywhere. It avoids getting embroiled in heated political controversies raging in Washington, D.C.. Located in Irvington-on-Hudson, New York, FEE has remained a purely education organization.

Since 1956, FEE has published *The Freeman*, an award-winning monthly journal with a long and noble lineage. Under the profound editorship of Paul Poirot it rose to great heights, always fighting for the timeless principles of the free society.

The *Freeman Classics* series reflects these heights, consisting of topical collections of great essays and articles published throughout the years. *Politicized Medicine* is the fifth volume in the series. Also available: *The Morality of Capitalism, Private Property and Political Control, Prices and Price Controls*, and *Education and Indoctrination*.

—Hans F. Sennholz